Advance Praise for

Steps for Writers
Composing Essays
Volume 2

"I think that my students would find the style appealing and at their reading level . . . The writing is stylistically consistent."
—Debra Favre, *Mt. San Antonio College*

"It has a generous, warm feel to me that I think students would respond to favorably. This is a good, solid composition text. It presents a more in-depth approach to writing theory and philosophy."
—Marcella Remund, *University of South Dakota*

"Eggers connects complexity of thought with good writing. I like it better than most developmental texts as it really goes for teaching writing and grammar. It's a good lead-in to higher level writing classes. This one seems more approachable, friendly, and less prescriptive than many (other texts)."
—Jennifer Black, *McLennan Community College*

"The writing style in *Steps for Writers* shows care, thought, and originality in use of language to craft sentences, with correct and varied structure."
—Torria Norman, *Black Hawk College*

About the Author

A native of Indiana, Philip Eggers received his A.B., M.A., and Ph.D. in English from Columbia University. He is professor and chairperson of the English Department at Borough of Manhattan Community College of the City University of New York, where for many years he has taught developmental writing and composition, as well as English, American, and world literature. As department chair, he helped  create the Writing and Literature Program at BMCC, which is nourishing much undergraduate writing talent. Professor Eggers was elected co-chair of the CUNY English Discipline Council, participated in a CUNY Mellon Seminar and two NEH Summer Seminars. He has presented at such forums as the CUNY CAWS (City University Association of Writing Supervisors) conferences and NEMLA (Northeast Modern Language Association). He is also a member of Phi Beta Kappa. In addition to a book on Tennyson and articles on English and American literature, he has written textbooks, including *Writing Skillful Sentences* and *Process and Practice*. Currently Professor Eggers is teaching, writing, and administering a department, but his chief preoccupations are being a father and grandfather, jogging, exploring global literature, and finding time to travel.

Steps for Writers

Composing Essays
Volume 2

Philip Eggers

Borough of Manhattan Community College
The City University of New York

PENGUIN ACADEMICS

PEARSON
Longman

New York   San Francisco   Boston
London   Toronto   Sydney   Tokyo   Singapore   Madrid
Mexico City   Munich   Paris   Cape Town   Hong Kong   Montreal

Vice President and Editor in Chief: Joseph Terry
Acquisitions Editor: Melanie Craig
Marketing Manager: Thomas DeMarco
Senior Supplements Editor: Donna Campion
Production Manager: Savoula Amanatidis
Project Coordination, Text Design, and Electronic Page Makeup: Electronic
Publishing Services Inc., NYC
Cover Design Manager: Nancy Danahy
Cover Image: © Iconica/Getty Images, Inc.
Senior Manufacturing Buyer: Dennis Para
Printer and Binder: R. R. Donnelly and Sons Company—Harrisonburg
Cover Printer: Phoenix Color Corporation

For more information about the Penguin Academics series, please contact us
by mail at Longman Publishers, attn. Marketing Department, 1185 Avenue of
the Americas, 25th Floor, New York, NY 10036, or by e-mail at
www.ablongman.com.

For permission to use copyrighted material, grateful acknowledgment is made
to the copyright holders on pp. 249–250, which are hereby made part of this
copyright page.

Library of Congress Cataloging-in-Publication Data

Eggers, Philip.
    Steps for writers : composing essays, volume 2 / Philip Eggers.
        p.   cm.
    Includes index.
    Includes bibliographical references and index.
    ISBN 0-321-19882-4
    1. English language—Rhetoric.   2. English language—Grammar—
Problems, exercises, etc.   3. Report writing—Problems, exercises, etc.
I. Title.
    PE1408.E3595 2006
    808'.042--dc22

                                                2006021405

Please visit us at www.ablongman.com.

ISBN 0-321-19882-4

        6 7 8 9 10—DOH—12 11

"I am convinced more and more day by day that fine writing is next to fine doing the top thing in the world."
—John Keats, letter to J. H. Reynolds, 24 August 1819

For Jane, a fine writer and the finest of doers.

Contents

STEP TWO WRITING ESSAYS BASED ON YOUR OWN EXPERIENCE AND PERCEPTIONS   75

STEP THREE WRITING ESSAYS BASED ON YOUR READING AND RESEARCH   127

CHAPTER 10   Making a Comparison   128

To the Instructor

Ours is an exciting and frustrating age in which to teach college writing. More students than ever hope to become novelists, poets, and journalists, but a small and shrinking percentage of students arrive at college with a mastery of basic skills and a rich vocabulary. The disparity between aspirations and aptitude has never been wider. In the past, writing instructors, knowing that many students feared writing and were aware of their deficiencies, often felt the need to reassure students, to help them realize that they could learn to write competently if they could overcome their anxieties. For some students, of course, such anxiety will remain the chief problem. Today's generation of undergraduates, however, have grown up instant-messaging one another and witnessing books written by untrained authors becoming best-sellers. A new problem, then, added to the lack of confidence that troubles some students, is the overconfidence of others. Many do not believe they need writing instruction, either because they think they already know how to write or because they expect someone else to edit and proofread their work.

The graduated approach of *Steps for Writers* is designed to cope with both problems. Students whose confidence needs to be bolstered can begin with basic exercises and assignments that are easy enough to manage. They will be able to experience success before confronting more difficult tasks. Students who are impatient and overconfident will face the reality check of exercises and assignments that will challenge their overconfidence while allowing them to move forward quickly in areas where they are genuinely proficient.

Because every student writer is different, texts and instructors must be flexible. You may choose to follow the sequence of chapters in *Steps for Writers* as the basis for a syllabus, but many instructors prefer not to structure their course on the table of contents of any text. Although you will probably want to follow the general progression of the three major "steps," the sequence of chapters within each step need not be taken as strictly chronological. The experience of learning to write has often been described as recursive, and any book or course should recognize the cycles and repetitions inherent in the process, while at the same time always emphasizing the large goal of growth and development. The definition of one mode as more advanced than another has to be somewhat arbitrary, as narrative can be highly complex and argumentation can be simple. Nevertheless, it is usually easier for students to write experiential essays before engaging in textual analysis or research writing.

Steps for Writers is based on the assumption that we are teaching writing as a means of learning, perhaps as the most important activity in students' intellectual maturation. The importance of writing in recent years has been underscored by state legislatures enacting laws requiring writing in public colleges, by university systems mandating mid-level proficiency tests, and by the SAT and other tests incorporating writing assessment in the measures used for college admissions. Writing Across the Curriculum has become standard practice in nearly every university. There has been a concomitant emphasis on critical thinking in composition pedagogy, no doubt because we perceive that students are vulnerable to the worst kinds of bias and manipulation, from the blandishments of advertising and the specious claims of political leaders to the urban legends found on Web sites. Along with the emphasis on critical thinking, however, we should incorporate the equally important element of creative writing not just in courses labeled Creative Writing, but in academic and career writing as well. Being able to propose solutions to problems, formulate original thesis statements, and employ vivid, resourceful diction and style requires creative thinking analogous to the inventiveness displayed by poets and novelists. Fiction and poetry in turn also involve critical thinking. Resisting the tendency to bifurcate critical and creative writing, *Steps for Writers* encourages students to take an interest in both aspects of their writing and incorporates some fiction and poetry among other kinds of professional writing as prose models.

Students are likely to feel empowered and to enjoy their writing more if their logical and imaginative faculties are brought out conjointly.

Acknowledgments

I am deeply grateful to the following professors who, by their comments, have made this a better textbook: Debra Favre of Mt. San Antonio College, Marcella Remund of the University of South Dakota–Sioux Falls, and Torria Norman of Black Hawk College.

I am indebted as well to the Allyn & Bacon/Longman editors who have contributed indispensably to the project, including Steve Rigolosi, Frederick Speers, Susan Kunchandy, Melanie Craig, and Lindsey Allen. I owe much to my colleagues and students at the Borough of Manhattan Community College, from whom I have learned most of what I know about teaching and whose advice and examples have taught me so much about all aspects of writing. Most of all, I wish to thank Jane J. Young, my life partner, for sharing with me all the joys and problems of teaching composition and literature and all the vicissitudes of life.

TEXT-SPECIFIC SUPPLEMENTS

An Instructor's Manual/Test Bank (ISBN 0-321-19886-7) is available to adopters. Contact your local Longman sales representative for a copy.

The Longman Developmental English Package

Longman is pleased to offer a variety of support materials to help make teaching developmental English easier on teachers and to help students excel in their coursework. Many of our student supplements are available at no additional cost or at a greatly reduced price when packaged with *Steps for Writers*. Contact your local Longman sales representative for more information on pricing and how to create a package.

Additional Support Materials for Writing Instructors

Printed Test Bank for Developmental Writing
(Instructor / ISBN 0-321-08486-1)

Features more than 5,000 questions in all areas of writing, from grammar to paragraphing through essay writing, research, and documentation.

Electronic Test Bank for Developmental Writing
(Instructor / CD ISBN 0-321-08117-X)

Features more than 5,000 questions in all areas of writing, from grammar to paragraphing through essay writing, research, and documentation. Instructors simply choose questions from the electronic test bank and then print out the completed test for distribution or instead offer the test online.

Diagnostic and Editing Tests, Sixth Edition
(Instructor / Print ISBN 0-321-19647-3 / CD ISBN 0-321-19645-7)

This collection of diagnostic tests helps instructors assess students' competence in standard written English to determine placement or to gauge progress.

The Longman Guide to Classroom Management
(Instructor / ISBN 0-321-09246-5)

This guide is designed as a helpful resource for instructors who have classroom management problems. It includes helpful strategies for dealing with disruptive students in the classroom and the do's and don'ts of discipline.

The Longman Guide to Community Service-Learning in the English Classroom and Beyond
(Instructor / ISBN 0-321-12749-8)

Written by Elizabeth Rodriguez Kessler of California State University—Northridge, this monograph provides a definition and history of service-learning, as well as an overview of how service-learning can be integrated effectively into the college classroom.

For Writing Students

The Longman Writer's Portfolio and Student Planner (ISBN 0-321-29609-5)

This unique supplement provides students with a space to plan, think about, and present their work. In addition to the yearly planner, this portfolio includes an assessing/organizing area (including a grammar diagnostic test, a spelling quiz, and project planning worksheets), a before and during writing area (including peer review sheets, editing checklists, writing self-evaluations, and a personal editing profile), and an after-writing area (including a progress chart, a final table of contents, and a final assessment), as well as a daily planner for students including daily, weekly, and monthly calendars.

Longman English Tutor Center Access Card (Value Pack: ISBN 0-201-71049-8 or Stand Alone: ISBN 0-201-72170-8)

This unique service offers students access to an in-house writing tutor via phone and/or e-mail. Tutor is available from 5PM–12AM Sun.–Thurs.

The Longman Writer's Journal, Mimi Markus (Student / ISBN 0-321-08639-2)

The book provides students with their own personal space for writing and contains helpful journal writing strategies, sample journal entries by other students, and many writing prompts and topics to get students writing.

ESL Worksheets, Third Edition (Student / ISBN 0-321-07765-2)

These worksheets provide ESL students with extra practice in areas they find the most troublesome. Diagnostic tests, suggested writing topics, and an answer key are included.

Peer Evaluation Manual, Seventh Edition (Student / ISBN 0-321-01948-2)

The manual offers students forms for peer critiques, general guidelines, and specific forms for different stages in the writing process and for various types of papers.

Learning Together
(Student / ISBN 0-673-46848-8)
This brief guide to the fundamentals of collaborative learning teaches students how to work effectively in groups.

Longman Editing Exercises
(Student / ISBN 0-205-31792-8)
These 54 pages of paragraph editing exercises provide students extra practice using grammar skills in the context of longer passages.

100 Things to Write About
(Student / ISBN 0-673-98239-4)
This brief book contains over 100 individual writing assignments on a variety of topics and in a wide range of formats, from expressive to analytical writing.

Research Navigator Guide for English, H. Eric Branscomb
& Doug Gotthoffer
(Student / ISBN 0-321-20277-5)
Designed to teach students how to conduct high-quality online research and to document it properly, *Research Navigator* provides discipline-specific academic resources, in addition to helpful tips on the writing process, online research, and finding and citing valid sources. *Research Navigator Guide* includes an access code to *Research Navigator*™—providing access to thousands of academic journals and periodicals, the NY Times Search by Subject Archive, Link Library, Library Guides, and more.

Penguin Discount Novel Program
In cooperation with Penguin Putnam, Inc., Longman is proud to offer a variety of Penguin paperbacks at a significant discount when packaged with any Longman title. Excellent additions to any English course, Penguin titles provide students the opportunity to explore contemporary and classical fiction and drama. The available titles include works by authors as diverse as Toni Morrison, Julia Alvarez, Mary Shelley, and Shakespeare. To review the complete list of titles available, visit the Longman-Penguin-Putnam website: http://www.ablongman.com/penguin.

The New American Webster Handy College Dictionary
(Student / ISBN 0-451-18166-2)
This paperback reference text has more than 100,000 entries.

Oxford American College Dictionary
(Student / ISBN 0-399-14415-3)
Drawing on Oxford's unparalleled language resources, including a 200-million-word database, this college dictionary contains more than 175,000 entries and more than 1,000 illustrations, including line drawings, photographs, and maps. *It is available at a significant discount when packaged with a Longman textbook.*

The Oxford American Desk Dictionary and Thesaurus,
Second Edition
(ISBN 0-425-18068-9)
From the Oxford University Press and Berkley Publishing Group comes this one-of-a-kind reference book that combines both of the essential language tools—dictionary and thesaurus—in a single, integrated A-to-Z volume. The 1,024-page book offers more than 150,000 entries, definitions, and synonyms so you can find the right word every time, as well as appendixes of valuable quick-reference information including: signs and symbols, weights and measures, presidents of the United States, states and capitals, and more.

The Oxford Essential Thesaurus
(ISBN 0-425-16421-7)
From Oxford University Press, renowned for quality educational and reference works, comes this concise, easy-to-use thesaurus—the essential tool for finding just the right word for every occasion. The 528-page book includes 175,000 synonyms in a simple A-to-Z format, more than 10,000 entries, extensive word choices, example sentences and phrases, and guidance on usage, punctuation, and more in the exclusive "Writers Toolkit."

Multimedia Offerings

Interested in incorporating online materials into your course? Longman is happy to help. Our regional technology specialists provide training on all of our multimedia offerings.

MyWritingLab

MyWritingLab is a complete online learning program that offers better practice to make better writers for college and life. The mastery-based format allows multiple attempts so students can learn from mistakes and build a solid foundation of writing principles. MyWritingLab provides:

- *Progressive Learning Exercises:* The exercises move from literal comprehension to critical application to demonstrating concepts in actual writing. This progressive learning process helps to transfer the skills into writing.

- *Easy Planning:* Based on the book chosen for the course and the work done in MyWritingLab, the system will generate an easy-to-use Study Plan.

- *A Comprehensive Exercises Program:* The 9,000 exercises include grammar, paragraph development, essay development, and research.

- *Diagnostic Testing:* A comprehensive diagnostic test assesses students' understanding of grammar and reflects the areas where help is needed most.

- *Easy Progress Tracking:* The My Gradebook enables students to monitor and track work done in MyWritingLab.

- *Access to Additional Valuable Resources:* our English Tutor Center, the interactive Study Skills Website, and the Research Navigator™.

Visit http://www.mywritinglab.com/ for more information and a video walkthrough.

STATE SPECIFIC SUPPLEMENTS

For Florida Adopters

Thinking Through the Test: A Study Guide for the Florida College Basic Skills Exit Test, D. J. Henry (For Florida Adoptions Only). This workbook helps students strengthen their reading skills in preparation for the Florida College Basic Skills Exit Test. It features both diagnostic tests to help assess areas that may need improvement and exit tests to help test skill mastery.

Detailed explanatory answers have been provided for almost all of the questions. *Package item only—not available for sale.*

Available Versions

Thinking Through the Test, A Study Guide for the Florida College Basic Skills Exit Tests: Reading and Writing, with Answer Key, Third Edition (ISBN 0-321-38739-2)

Thinking Through the Test, A Study Guide for the Florida College Basic Skills Exit Tests: Reading and Writing (without Answer Key), Third Edition (ISBN 0-321-38740-6)

Thinking Through the Test, A Study Guide for the Florida College Basic Skills Exit Tests: Writing, with Answer Key, Third Edition (ISBN 0-321-38741-4)

Thinking Through the Test, A Study Guide for the Florida College Basic Skills Exit Tests: Writing (without Answer Key), Third Edition (ISBN 0-321-38934-4)

Writing Skills Summary for the Florida State Exit Exam, D. J. Henry
(Student / ISBN 0-321-08477-2) (For Florida Adoptions Only). An excellent study tool for students preparing to take Florida College Basic Skills Exit Test for Writing, this laminated writing grid summarizes all the skills tested on the Exit Exam. *Package item only—not available for sale.*

CLAST Test Package, Fourth Edition
(Instructor / Print ISBN 0-321-01950-4)
These two, 40-item objective tests evaluate students' readiness for the Florida CLAST exams. Strategies for teaching CLAST preparedness are included.

For Texas Adopters

The Longman THEA Study Guide, Jeannette Harris
(Student / ISBN 0-321-27240-0)
Created specifically for students in Texas, this study guide includes straightforward explanations and numerous practice exercises to help students prepare for the reading and writing sections of THEA Test. *Package item only—not available for sale.*

TASP Test Package, Third Edition
(Instructor / Print ISBN 0-321-01959-8)

These 12 practice pre-tests and post-tests assess the same reading and writing skills covered in the Texas TASP examination.

For New York/CUNY Adopters

Preparing for the CUNY-ACT Reading and Writing Test, edited by Patricia Licklider
(Student / ISBN 0-321-19608-2)

This booklet, prepared by reading and writing faculty from across the CUNY system, is designed to help students prepare for the CUNY-ACT exit test. It includes test-taking tips, reading passages, typical exam questions, and sample writing prompts to help students become familiar with each portion of the test.

Philip Eggers
Borough of Manhattan Community College
The City University of New York

To the Student

The Steps Approach

Like all writers, you will learn to write in your unique way, and your best writing will bear the stamp of your individuality. There are steps you or any writer should take, however, to learn how to write effective essays and develop good writing habits. This book is designed to help you take those steps and experience the satisfaction of writing correctly and with focus, precision, clarity, and originality. Climbing steps sounds like work—and learning to write better does take work—but as you improve, writing will also become more enjoyable. Your enriched vocabulary and increased command of sentence structure and style will give you greater confidence. Freed from the embarrassment of making frequent basic errors, and experienced at developing and organizing your ideas, you will become a more creative and interesting writer.

As you do the individual assignments and exercises in this book, keep an eye on your long-term progress. Learning to write requires a lot of repetition, but the repetition occurs at higher and higher levels. Sometimes it may seem that you are going backward because you find yourself confused about some features of grammar that you have already studied. At other times you may seem to be standing still because you repeat the same mistakes. These feelings stem from the fact that as you take on more challenging writing assignments and acquire more vocabulary, you will be operating on a higher level, where such matters as sentence structure, agreement of subject and verb, and use of pronouns become more challenging. The three-step grammar and writing exercises will remind you to keep applying what you have learned as you progress to more advanced work.

Organization

Because this book is arranged in a series of three "steps," with graduated exercises in each chapter, your instructor will probably want you to follow the sequence of units as they are presented. Although there may be exceptions, depending on your particular course and instructor, it makes sense to move in the general direction from Step One through Steps Two and Three. Step One introduces you to the whole writing process, which every writer shapes for his or her own use. Step Two involves writing essays based mostly on your own experience and what you already know of the world around you—your family, friends, school, job, and teams and organizations to which you belong. These compositions do not require extensive use of texts or research, and therefore are the kind of work your instructor may want you to do for your first formal essays. Step Three follows logically from Step Two, with assignments and exercises based on writing that incorporates either texts that you read or research materials that you find.

While *Steps for Writers* is arranged sequentially with an eye to your developing skills, its structure is flexible so that it can be used in a variety of ways. For instance, some courses may lack sufficient time to complete all the chapters. Or, your instructor may wish to arrange the assignments differently, which can be readily accomplished because the order of individual chapters within each step can easily be changed. Remember, too, that if chapters or exercises are omitted from your class assignments, you can still learn a lot by studying them on your own. More than your instructors or your textbooks, you are the one in charge of your own learning. As you take ownership of your own writing, you will learn faster and enjoy it more.

Special Features

A graduated approach. *Steps for Writers* has a number of features designed to help you achieve success as a writer, beginning with its graduated approach to both grammar and composition. Learning to write essays is not like learning chemistry or Russian, where every lesson introduces you to totally new information. You are, after all, writing in a language you already know, even if it is not your first language. Consequently, the knowledge and skills you acquire are not easy to identify and separate from what you already know. In fact, you may have some previously learned misinformation and bad habits that need to be corrected. For that reason you will not always be able to detect your steady advancement as a writer. The arrangement of large and small steps in this book will help you recognize that what sometimes seems like sliding backward is actually an upward climb that will carry you to a higher place.

Before each set of grammar exercises, you will find a Test Yourself exercise that you can do as a follow-up to the grammar lesson. The answers are provided for these exercises so that you can see how well you understand that feature of grammar before you begin the graduated exercises. You will probably find the first step, the basic exercise, fairly easy. At times you may also find that you can do the intermediate and challenge exercises successfully. At other times, however, the intermediate and challenge exercises may be just that—a challenge. Do not be discouraged; very few people have a perfect command of all aspects of grammar. When you have difficulties, be ready to do extra work and seek a tutor if necessary. But do not expect every level to be easy: if it were, you would already be an advanced writer with very little need for instruction or textbooks!

Student models and professional essays. The student models in each chapter will offer you examples of the kinds of writing students actually do—competent, well organized, and well written, but not beyond what you are capable of doing yourself. Of course, they are not meant for you to copy too closely but to recognize the features of good writing that you as a college student can expect of yourself. Sometimes you may find yourself writing better than the student models, at least in some features. The professional examples will provide texts for you to interpret, analyze, and discuss. You should use them as prose models that demonstrate the range of possibilities in different writing modes. You may be inspired to write better by witnessing how some of the best writers work, just as young athletes learn by watching professionals and Olympians. Sometimes you will find that your best writing is not all that different from the work of published authors, that you have some of the originality and insight they display. Instead of saying to yourself, "I could never do that," you may find yourself thinking, "I can do that myself." That's when writing really becomes enjoyable and you know you are learning.

Embedded proofreading exercises. Grammar is important. However, that doesn't mean you have to study every aspect of grammar from the ground up. As a college student you already know many rules and patterns of English grammar through habit, or, possibly, from instruction in high school. Unfortunately, unless you are a rare exception, that does not mean you can write without making mistakes. Although you probably don't need a whole course in grammar, you probably still have a few things to learn. On that assumption, this book is designed to incorporate grammar exercises as part of the proofreading process, which should come in the last stage of revision. For quick reference to specific grammatical topics, however, the index at the back will help you find whatever you need to know about fragments, spelling, subject-verb agreement, and so on.

Peer review questions. Your instructor will probably include some small-group work in your writing class or encourage you to share your work with others in a group outside class. Even when your courses do not require you to study with other students in a small group, such study will help you make a habit of sharing your writing with other writers. No writer can predict with any certainty how readers will respond to his or her work; usually some readers will give you helpful advice about how to make your work clearer, more interesting, or more convincing. It takes courage to listen to your classmates' responses, but you'll be glad you did. Each chapter of *Steps for Writers* contains peer review questions that you can use to elicit helpful responses to your writing in the particular mode involved. Use as many of these questions as you can; the answers will probably help you revise and enjoy your writing.

Arrangement by rhetorical modes. The rhetorical modes are the categories of writing that have been identified for many generations as different ways of developing material. Unlike the mythical Procrustes, who chopped off his visitors' feet if they were too tall to fit his bed or stretched them if they were too short, we should not try to make essays "fit" perfectly into one mold. However, composing essays in different modes will ensure that you experiment with a wide variety of writing. Like cross-training in a gym, diverse writing approaches will introduce you to varied kinds of thinking as well as varied ways of using language. Even your grammar skills will be tested differently when you are writing a narrative essay (telling a story) than when you are writing an argumentative essay.

Writing Tips. The 15 writing tips are intended to give you small but important reminders about tactics you should use in each chapter. They are not extended lessons but highlight some of the do's and don'ts at the core of each lesson. You will pick up other tips from your fellow students and instructors as you advance. It might be a good idea to keep a master list of what you learn about your steps to effective writing—the hints that you need to remember to avoid your habitual weaknesses and build on your strengths.

Above all, enjoy your writing. There is no gratification quite like writing well and sharing it with your readers.

Philip Eggers
Borough of Manhattan Community College
The City University of New York

INTRODUCTION
VISUALIZING THE ESSAY

Students often ask, "How can I learn to write a good essay?" That is the question this book is designed to answer. But no book can give you a blueprint for the many kinds of essays you may write in college. Just what is an essay? If you already have a notion of what an essay should be, your idea is probably at least partly right, because essays can take so many forms.

When the essay was invented—its inventor is often identified as the seventeenth-century French writer Michel de Montaigne—readers understood that the word *essay* meant "to try": an essay was an *attempt* to do something, an *effort* to explore a topic. An essay was considered worth writing even if the author didn't say everything possible on the subject, so long as he or she put in the effort to explore it. Today, a college essay is still an adventure in ideas, and it requires the same willingness as in Montaigne's day to explore ideas with effort and an open mind. How, then, can you write a good essay? Do not look for a formula, but be ready to work and be receptive to any facts or ideas that emerge. The right attitude and an effective approach are more important than any blueprint.

There is, however, a classic form for a college essay, which may help you when you begin writing. Among the many forms of the essay, most follow a familiar three-part structure:

INTRODUCTION: The introduction is a paragraph, or maybe two, that arouses readers' interest in the topic and gives them a clear idea of what you plan to say in the essay. It should begin with a short statement or question that evokes interest, and then continue with several sentences that lead up to a clear, forceful **thesis statement**, which announces your essay's main point. The thesis statement is often the last sentence in the introduction.

BODY: The body of an essay contains several paragraphs, usually three to five, that develop the main point. In this book you will study different ways to develop your points, using description, narration, comparison, persuasion, and so on. Each body paragraph may contain a **topic sentence** that acts as a signpost to guide the reader by introducing the subject of the paragraph. Learning to develop body paragraphs and connect them with transition words is a major part of learning to write essays.

CONCLUSION: Think of the conclusion as your introduction in reverse. You may begin by restating your thesis (though not in exactly the same words). Then find a way to end with interesting statements that leave food for further thought while remaining close to your main idea. Your last sentence, like the first one in your introduction, should be memorable and emphatic—and preferably short.

The description above may make it look as if the parts of an essay are just piled on top of one another. But the adventure of writing an essay is not like stacking cans in a grocery; it is more like exploring a neighborhood—one that you are acquainted with but that also contains many surprises. As you move from one part of your essay to the next, say to yourself, "This idea leads me to another point, and that point makes me realize that. . . ." An essay is a kind of guided tour from one idea to another. Every paragraph topic should follow from the previous one, and every sentence lead to the next. This sequence of ideas and statements is the glue that holds the essay together on the inside and makes the organization of your essay visible "from the outside" to the reader.

Of course, creating an essay that develops out of itself and moves smoothly from beginning to end is not always quick and easy. Writers have many ways of creating essays, progressing from one stage to another from their first ideas through numerous drafts and revisions to a final completed and corrected composition. We call these methods of creating essays the *writing process*, which also involves a process of thinking and learning. To write well, you will have to discover your own version of the *writing process*.

The essay below is the final product at the end of one student's writing process. First, to understand what an essay is, let's examine it as a completed whole. Later, we can follow the steps author Sarah Chen took in getting to her completed work.

Student Essay

The essay below is the kind that supports a main point by illustrating several supporting points, or subtopics. Although this is one of the most common forms used in academic writing, it isn't the only one. This essay is a revised and edited draft. In the section on revising your work, you will see some of the steps the writer took to arrive at her final version.

Why Liberal Arts?

Sarah Chen

Introduction

Our sociology teacher once asked the class a difficult question. She wanted to know whether we would rather have our college degree without the education or the education without the degree. Most of the students decided that they would rather have the degree, because the jobs they wanted required college degrees. Other students, including me, argued that, in the long run, knowledge is more important than a meaningless piece of paper. We didn't settle the argument, but we had to think a lot about what an education, particularly a liberal arts education, is for. With so much emphasis on career training, we wondered, why should students spend time taking courses that aren't required in their nursing or engineering curriculum? *We came up with some good reasons why a liberal arts education is more important than ever.*

Thesis Statement

Topic Sentence

First, there is the question of careers. Students often make the mistake of thinking they will succeed by getting narrow training for a specific job without acquiring a good general education. They want to earn a lot of money in a hurry, and sometimes they do. When computers first came on the scene, people who trained as computer scientists and programmers often made a lot of money, sometimes even without any higher education. But then the job market in computers shrank, as jobs were sent overseas, and many of those well-paid workers were laid off. They had no other training or education to fall back on. In the long run, a person with a broad education will be much better able to change jobs and adapt to new technologies than someone with a narrower background.

Supporting Example

Topic Sentence

Another reason why a good liberal arts education matters is that it promotes participation in society. Jobs and salaries are important, but they are not a person's whole life. Most people gain a great deal from their activities in local organizations, labor unions, religious institutions, political causes, and other associations. If fewer and fewer people achieve a broad education, our social institutions will suffer. Where will we get the scout leaders, PTA officers, neighborhood spokespersons, and even intelligent voters? Education is not just for the benefit of the individual; it is also necessary for the good of society.

Support by Explaining an Effect

Topic Sentence

People need to be broadly educated for the sake of their families as well. Most parents want their children to achieve at least as much as they have accomplished and have at least as good a lifestyle. Knowing about psychology helps parents raise emotionally healthy children, and knowing about many subjects allows parents to guide their children's education. As well-educated people, they set

Support by Analyzing a Process

better examples for their sons and daughters, causing them to set higher goals for themselves. Since many children do not follow the same careers as their fathers and mothers, parents will be better able to communicate with their children if they know something about the careers they are interested in pursuing.

Topic Sentence

Finally, a good education helps individuals to cultivate their own talents. One of the greatest satisfactions in life is the expression of one's own creativity. My aunt, who has just retired from her job as a bank manager, has begun writing poems and composing music for them. She studied music and literature in college but never had time to do much more than listen to concerts and read poetry and novels while she was working. She wrote some poems, but now that she has more time, she is writing a lot of them and composing songs. And she has actually gotten several songs chosen by record companies to be included on CDs by well-known artists. Her success is giving her as much fun and satisfaction as her job ever did. She wouldn't have been able to be creative without a good liberal arts education.

Support with Personal Experience

Conclusion

All of these reasons won't be enough to stop some students from choosing narrow technical training and ignoring their overall education. But many of those who do will probably regret their choice later and may go back and take courses in subjects they missed out on when they were younger. Luckily, it is possible nowadays to get all sorts of courses online or at local colleges, no matter how old you are. *In whatever way you get it, however, a liberal arts education has a lot of advantages.*

Restatement of Thesis

In the essay above, identify the following: 1) the main idea 2) supporting points 3) transition words 4) methods of developing supporting points.

Like most successful essays, this essay has a clear main point, subtopics, and overall structure. In your writing, try to follow the principles illustrated here: state a clear main thesis, develop it in paragraphs that contain supporting material, use transition words and topic sentences to guide the reader, and tie your thoughts together at the end. This essay is also successful because it takes a stand. Which of Sarah's statements do you find most convincing? Which are least convincing? Can you think of a counter argument? What could someone say on the opposite side?

STEP ONE

DEVELOPING YOUR OWN THINKING, WRITING, AND LEARNING PROCESS

CHAPTER 1
PREWRITING

Imagine a tower with spiral staircase inside. Visualize yourself climbing this staircase and looking out a series of windows one above the other. At first, the windows are so near the ground you do not see much of the landscape below, but each time you reach a higher window, the same view, seen from a higher perspective, opens up an ever-expanding prospect. Climbing the steps takes effort, and the view sometimes seems not to change much from one level to the next. But by the time you have reached the top, your efforts reward you with a grander panorama than you could ever have imagined when taking your first steps.

Learning to write is a little like that. It often seems repetitious. It takes effort. You may hear yourself complaining, "Thesis statements again? Subject-verb agreement—I've done that! Why am I still having trouble with verb tenses?" But each time you repeat a topic, you do so at a higher and higher level as you gain new vocabulary, learn to write with increasing maturity, learn to vary sentences, and take up the challenge of difficult academic topics. In Langston Hughes's poem "Mother to Son" a wise woman says to her son, "Life for me ain't been no crystal stair." Again, this is true of writing: It will not always be easy, and sometimes you will feel like sitting down on the steps, but as you improve, you will find increasing satisfaction in all stages of the writing process.

Writing is a process of thinking and learning. Accomplished writers often say that many of their best ideas come to them *while* they are writing, not beforehand. Writing a paper on an aspect of psychology or history is often the best way to understand and remember information on the subject. Learning is both passive and active; it is part taking in and remembering, and part organizing, analyzing, and expressing. When you develop your unique writing process, you will also be developing your powers of thinking and learning.

And what is this mysterious writing process? Like all writers you will find a unique way of making the journey from the first steps of thinking about an idea for a writing project to creating, revising, and touching up your completed work. Experiment and find the methods that work best for you. Everybody is a little different. But, for most writers, there are roughly three main steps in the writing process:

- The many kinds of **preliminary activities** they go through before they get down to systematic composing, many of which are as much about thinking as writing;

- The **composing** process itself, which entails varied modes of organization; and

- The process of looking over their work, **revising**, and **correcting**.

Prewriting Experiments: Freewriting, Focused Writing, Brainstorming, Clustering, Outlining, and Cubing

A number of techniques have been developed to help writers get started, especially those troubled by writer's block. On any specific assignment, certain techniques will work better than others, and you can experiment with the ones described here to see which work best for you. **Freewriting** and **focused writing** are methods of nonstop writing that you do without pausing or self-censoring. Keep writing for five minutes or until you fill up two pages. Using these methods will not produce a masterpiece, or even an essay, but it may make you less inhibited so that you will begin to write fluently, the way you talk in conversation. The main difference between freewriting and focused writing is that you do the first while letting your mind wander on any subject that occurs to you—just free associate. Focused writing, on the other hand, requires you to stay on one general subject, such as television, sports, your appearance, shopping, politics, or college courses.

Brainstorming is a method best used in a group of people and involves tossing ideas around for consideration, coming up with anything relevant to the topic. This method is particularly helpful for writers whose words flow easily during speech but who do not put enough thought into their writing. Brainstorming will help you if you have trouble making your essays interesting and original, especially if you brainstorm with other lively, talkative people. On the other hand, brainstorming produces an abundance of chaotic facts and ideas. If you mainly have trouble *organizing* material, follow up your brainstorming with activities that help you organize.

Clustering, for instance, is a popular activity that might help you arrange material into groups of subtopics. It is a process of sorting your facts and thoughts into groups, or clusters, by writing them inside balloons such as the ones you see in cartoons. A cluster gives you a picture of your topic, with its main concept at the center and subordinate ideas branching off from it, like this:

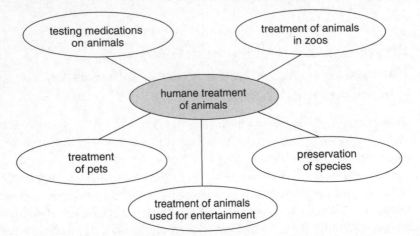

Clustering helps you recognize your essay's main topic, the secondary topics, and the supporting details. If you often mix up important points with unimportant details, clustering is for you.

An old-fashioned method of planning an essay is to use **outlining**. Some writers resist such neat, detailed planning, because they believe that it may stifle creativity. If you're one of those people, freewriting or focused writing is probably the best way for you to begin. But if you're the kind of writer who follows every turnoff and loses the main highway, so to speak, outlining may give you the map you need to keep moving in the right direction. If you use outlines frequently, be ready to adjust them between drafts: Ideas—good ideas—will occur to you as you write, and you may have to alter parts of your outline or even create a new outline.

Cubing sounds like geometry, doesn't it? A cube has six surfaces, and some writers like to use the term to remind themselves that not only do topics have many ideas and facts associated with them, but also that they can be seen from many perspectives. If you tend to see a topic from the same angle, cubing may be your most useful prewriting activity. A cube has six surfaces; try to envision a topic from six directions. Imagine you have to write about the World Wide Web and cannot think of enough angles. Try a cubing exercise using these six "sides" of the topic:

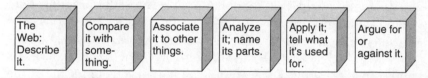

This kind of activity usually produces more ideas than you can possibly use in one essay, but if your problem is a one-track mind, cubing may help you develop more tracks and write more intelligent, mature essays.

Interacting with Your Readers

As you prepare to compose an essay, it is important that you think about interacting with your readers. You probably have strong ideas about your topic. Readers may agree or disagree with your ideas. To find out how others respond to your thoughts on the topic, read aloud some of your best focused writing and get feedback from a number of other people, either in your class writing group or at home. Notice unexpected responses such as points your readers disagree with or passages they find confusing, funny, or moving. Listen to suggestions for added points and examples. Your readers' responses provide a rich opportunity for you to make your writing moving and convincing. Your readers may catch a few mistakes as well.

Identifying Your Purpose

The transitional phase toward actually composing an essay is identifying your purpose in writing the essay. Every essay worth reading has a strong purpose. This purpose—whether it is to portray a person as a hero, compare one film with another, explain how to apply a software program, or persuade your readers to change their college curriculum—can always be summed up in a single statement or two. Often this summation takes the form of a thesis statement near the end of your first paragraph. You should always be able to answer the question, What are you trying to say in this essay? Knowing what you are trying to accomplish in your essay is essential to writing effectively, even though that purpose may change as you compose.

Prewriting Activities: A Glimpse of a Student Writer at Work

You've read Sarah Chen's essay in its final form. Like most writers, Sarah went through many steps to get to this final draft. First, her instructor asked the class to think up topics for essays on education. Working in groups, the students brainstormed categories that included the cost of education, education in other countries, problems with high schools in the U.S., athletics in college, fraternities and sororities, science education, training for jobs in business, the benefits of a college degree, the difference between community colleges and four-year colleges, and training for nursing and medicine.

The students agreed with the instructor that these topics were too broad and had to be narrowed. Sarah was particularly interested in the topic of community colleges, because she was attending a community college but wanted to complete a bachelor's degree later. Instead of trying to write an essay on the broad topic of the differences between two-year and four-year colleges, she decided to try some focused writing to explore her ideas. Here is some of what she wrote:

> Here I am in a community college. I'm not sure what I'm doing here, but I like my courses, well, most of them. Biology and English are interesting and Western Civilization is ok but we have too much memorizing of dates. I'm more interested in ideas. I'm good at math but my pre-calculus course is a bore, maybe because I had some of the material in high school. So far liberal arts is all right as a major because I can pick classes where I can learn things in different subjects and not have to be too narrow yet. Why do they call it liberal

arts? Gina told me in high school she wanted to go to a liberal arts college. I wonder what kind of job she'll get with a liberal arts degree. How did I get on this topic? I'm supposed to be comparing community colleges and four-year colleges. They both have liberal arts, whatever that is. I'm supposed to know. Maybe that would be a good topic to write about. My adviser asked me what I wanted to do in the future, what kind of career I wanted. I told her I wasn't sure but that I wanted to work with people.

That was pretty lame, but honestly I don't know yet. I don't think I want to be a nurse or a doctor. I'd rather work with healthy people than sick people. Maybe a teacher or a social worker. I want to make money but I would get bored just analyzing stocks and people's retirement accounts. On the other hand, if I don't make enough money I may not be very happy with the work I'm doing and want to change careers. My uncle told me last week that my generation should expect to have at least six jobs in our lifetimes and be ready to move from one job to another. That sounds scary. I'll have to have my resume updated all the time and get recommendation letters. It might be better if I try to do something where I won't have to change jobs every other year. But still I want to get a good education. There are too many interesting subjects for me to just choose one and stick to nothing but courses in that field now. I'm not ready to make up my mind yet. Besides, isn't that what you do in a four-year college?

Sarah continued her focused writing for several pages. Obviously, this kind of loose writing is not an essay, but it did help her realize that what she cared about is why she wanted to get a liberal arts degree. So, answering that question would be the main purpose of her essay. Next, she tried arranging her topic into a cluster:

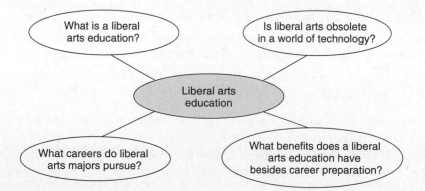

At this point it was possible for Sarah to organize her ideas into an outline that would provide the basis for the complete draft of an essay. Here is her outline:

Thesis: A liberal arts education is more important than ever in today's world.

I. People with liberal arts education contribute to society.

II. A liberal arts education enriches family life.

III. A liberal arts education makes an individual happier and more creative.

IV. Liberal arts is a good preparation for many careers.

Sarah decided at this point to write a rough draft of her essay without going into detail on each point, because she thought ideas would come to her as she wrote. As a result, her first draft was clearly organized but needed a lot of revision. See Chapter 4, on revision, to find out how she proceeded with her next steps.

WRITING TIP #1

Take the time to prewrite even when you feel impatient and want to begin composing the essay itself. Thinking and planning now will pay off in a better essay later. Remember: Once you compose your essay, you must be ready to revise it, but the more thinking and prewriting you do ahead of time, the more material you will have to work with. The best writers do *more* thinking, planning, drafting, and changing than weaker writers, not less.

Writing Exercises: Basic, Intermediate, Challenge

☐ Basic Exercise: Prewriting Experiments

Write for five minutes without stopping. Begin with the sentence, "Some things I like to do alone, but other things I enjoy doing with people." Do not worry about grammar, organization, or anything else—just write without hesitating. Keep writing as if you were dancing or doing aerobic exercises—like those activities, you gain the benefits of this work (developing fluency) only if you keep moving.

After you have written for five minutes, put your writing aside. Look at it later and see whether you can identify a strong idea that you expressed in the piece. Look also for clusters of ideas that might be organized into groups. Create a cluster diagram, a writing cube, or an outline based on the thoughts you have expressed in your freewriting.

■ Intermediate Exercise: Prewriting Experiments

Write without stopping until you've filled up two single-spaced pages. Begin with the sentence, "There are a number of things I would like to change about our society."

Try to stay focused on this general idea, but do not worry about grammar or being right about everything you say. The important thing is to develop a flow of words and ideas.

After putting this focused writing aside for a while, look at it again and try to find your most important idea—an opinion that holds your thoughts together. Then identify some subordinate ideas and make a cluster diagram, writing cube, or outline. Omit any topics that seem too far out of the main focus of your draft. Save this focused writing and other informal writing, such as journal entries, as possible sources for essay topics and supporting materials later.

■ Challenge Exercise: Prewriting Experiments

Write without stopping until you have two pages of thoughts about what you've learned in a course you are currently studying or have recently studied. Concentrate as in the previous exercises on writing without hesitating; do not puzzle over grammatical or factual details; just keep writing. As before, put your writing aside for a while, then look at it again. Search for the most important ideas and make a cluster, a writing cube, or an outline to help you identify a main thread of thought as well as supporting ideas. If there are ideas or facts that seem irrelevant to your most important opinions, omit them from the diagram or outline.

Proofreading Practice: Identifying Sentence Divisions in Your Prewriting Activities

Worrying too much about grammar is not appropriate when doing prewriting work. However, once you have substantial focused writing, look it over to see how well you control sentence structure. Experienced writers tend to write in complete sentences that are divided with correct punctuation marks, even when they are concentrating on the flow of ideas. Check your work to see whether you tend to write complete sentences and divide them correctly. If you find that you leave many **fragments**, **run-on sentences**, and **comma splices**, you may need a careful review of sentence grammar.

Avoid fragments, run-on sentences, and comma splices by dividing your sentences with the correct punctuation.

Correcting Fragments

Be sure all of your sentences are complete. Remember that every sentence must have a main clause, including a subject and verb that belong together. Remember, too, that a main clause cannot begin with connecting words such as *which, although, because, if,* or *when.* Main verbs cannot be *–ing* forms unless they have helping verbs. ("The person listening" is not a main clause, but "Sandra is listening" is a main clause.) Watch for the extra piece of a sentence that you tag on after completing a statement; it may belong with the sentence and need to be attached to it:

Fragment: Hector is an unusually careful person. <u>The kind of student who checks his work three times before turning it in.</u>

Correct: Hector is an unusually careful person<u>, the kind of student who checks his work three times before turning it in.</u>

Fragment: Jennifer signed up for Spanish II. <u>Even though she had never taken Spanish I.</u>

Correct: Jennifer signed up for Spanish II<u>, even though she had never taken Spanish I.</u>

Fragment: Tony took the turnoff for Route 84. <u>Which led to an entrance to the beltway.</u>

Correct: Tony took the turnoff for Route 84, <u>which led to an entrance to the beltway.</u>

Fragment: The film ended abruptly after the car chase. <u>And left the audience confused.</u>

Correct: The film ended abruptly after the car chase <u>and left the audience confused.</u>

TEST YOURSELF: CORRECT FRAGMENTS

Correct the fragments in the following examples:

1. Enid thought Homer was everything she wanted a boyfriend to be. A person who understood her, knew what she wanted, and shared her interests.

2. Teenagers often do not like to follow advice. Especially when it comes from their parents.

3. Marisol decided to visit Mexico in March. Whether her sister could go with her or not.

4. Steven usually reads the news on the Internet. And participates in three online discussion groups.

5. Her cousin is still a senior in high school. She has an associate's degree herself.

6. Playing golf requires strength, coordination, and concentration. Not to mention endurance.

7. The nutritionist recommended a low-fat, low-carb diet. As well as aerobic exercise three times a week.

Answers: 1. to be, a person who 2. advice, especially when 3. in March, whether her 4. the Internet and participates 5. correct 6. concentration, not to mention 7. diet, as well as

Correcting Run-on Sentences

Be careful to come to a full stop at the end of every sentence. If you run your sentences together without punctuation between them, they are harder to understand.

Incorrect: The members of the family came to the <u>reunion in May they also</u> went on a cruise of the Caribbean.

Correct: The members of the family came to the <u>reunion in May. They also</u> went on a cruise of the Caribbean.

Another possibility: The members of the family came to the <u>reunion. In May</u> they also went on a cruise of the Caribbean.

That is the problem with run-on sentences: They force the reader to figure out where one idea ends and the next begins. That's your job as the writer. Do not make the reader do it for you.

The way to correct run-on sentences is usually to find where the first sentence ends and place a period there. There are more complicated ways (see "Correcting Comma Splices" below), but let's practice with just dividing run-on sentences into two separate statements.

TEST YOURSELF: CORRECT RUN-ON SENTENCES

Correct the run-on sentences in the following examples:

1. Some of the exercises are designed to improve flexibility the last six are intended to build strength.

2. Five courses are available on Monday and Wednesday mornings which one would you prefer?

3. The smartest drivers are usually the ones who win in the end it all comes down to strategy.

4. Byron peered intently at the map for a moment. Then he stood up and gathered the bikers around him.

5. Sharon already knew how to play chess while living in Russia she became an expert.

6. Choosing the right digital camera can be complicated it depends on the kind of photographing you intend to do.

7. The sound track for Gerald's film begins with slow, quiet music suddenly it shifts into thunderous, chaotic noise.

Answers: 1. flexibility. The last 2. mornings. Which 3. who win. In the end
4. correct 5. play chess. While living 6. complicated. It depends 7. music.
Suddenly it

Correcting Comma Splices

Do not use commas in place of periods. When you get to the end
of a sentence and begin a new one, use a full stop. A semicolon (;)
can sometimes be used instead of the period.

Incorrect: The mother in this story tries her best to give her
daughter everything a child <u>needs, she</u> works hard to
provide food, shelter, and schooling.

Correct: The mother in this story tries her best to give her
daughter everything a child <u>needs. She</u> works hard to
provide food, shelter, and schooling.

Correct: The mother in this story tries her best to give her
daughter everything a child <u>needs; she</u> works hard to
provide food, shelter, and schooling.

You may also combine the two statements with the following
conjunctions:

, and   He was fond of Susan<u>, and</u> he wanted to marry her.

, or   You could go to college<u>, or</u> you could play the oboe.

, nor   She isn't happy in her job<u>, nor</u> does she like her apartment.

, but   The first part is easy<u>, but</u> the last section is a killer.

, yet   She liked the film<u>, yet</u> she thought it was too short.

, so   Sam was very hungry<u>, so</u> he ordered a pizza.

, for   No one could find the clue<u>, for</u> it was written in code.

Incorrect: The mother in this story tries her best to give her
daughter everything that she <u>needs, her</u> circumstances
make it impossible for her to give her daughter the
attention she craves.

Correct: The mother in this story tries her best to give her
daughter everything that she <u>needs, but her</u> circumstances make it impossible for her to give her daughter the attention she craves.

TEST YOURSELF: CORRECT COMMA SPLICES

Correct the comma splices in the following examples:

1. Some students put a lot of their life experiences into their essays, but others prefer not to write about their own lives.

2. The officers of the club made a mistake by calling meetings on Tuesday morning, many students have classes at that time.

3. The new job suits Barbara's schedule, it is only 20 hours a week and she has two days off.

4. The main character in this story reminds me of my girlfriend, she is too dependent on her family and controlled by their opinions.

5. Writing an essay requires planning and revision, you also have to do a lot of critical thinking.

6. The situations of the two mothers are similar, however, they respond to their problems of poverty and lack of support in different ways.

7. Some people do research on the Internet; others, who feel less comfortable with technology, still use only the library.

Answers: 1. correct 2. morning. Many students 3. schedule. It is 4. girlfriend. She is 5. revision. You also 6. similar. However, 7. correct

Proofreading Exercises: Basic, Intermediate, Challenge

☐ Basic Exercise: Sentence Divisions

Find the seven errors in the following passage. Rewrite the paragraph with corrections:

> Latoya decided to look for a new apartment, she wanted to have more space and a better view. Especially a view of the park. She first tried the old-fashioned system of looking in the newspapers for rental ads. There she found three apartments that sounded just right for her, she called all three of them immediately. Unfortunately, they had already been rented. Before she called. Then she thought about looking for an apartment on the Internet. After

doing a Web search. She found a list that had many inexpensive rentals. Just like the one she wanted. The second one she called was still available. She hurried over and looked at it. And was delighted to find the apartment of her dreams.

◼ Intermediate Exercise: Sentence Divisions

Find the seven errors in the following passage. Rewrite the paragraph with corrections:

Calvin thinks his economics course was the most interesting course he ever took. Because he learned so much about money, work, government programs, and corporations. Professor Wilson, who taught the course, really knew his subject. And knew how to present it to undergraduates. At first Calvin thought economics would be boring, he didn't know much about business and didn't like to work with statistics. The textbook was huge and expensive it looked difficult to read. After two weeks, however, he discovered that he could understand concepts like inflation, compound interest, and profit margins. As well as institutions like the Federal Reserve. At the beginning of the course he was a biology major, the course changed his mind about his course of studies and his career. Now he is thinking of taking a course in statistics he may even change his major to business administration.

◼ Challenge Exercise: Sentence Divisions

Find the seven errors in the following passage. Rewrite the paragraph with corrections:

Eileen read a story called "Roman Fever" by Edith Wharton, she liked it because of its surprise ending. The story tells about two upper-class widows from New York, Mrs. Slade and Mrs. Ansley, who have been friends for all of their adult lives. Although they seem to like and admire each other. Mrs. Slade envies Mrs. Ansley partly because her daughter is much livelier and more interesting than Mrs. Slade's daughter. But also because she suspects that Mr. Slade may have been secretly in love with Mrs. Ansley. The two women meet in Rome, they talk about an incident years ago before they married their husbands. Mrs. Slade wrote a letter to Mrs. Ansley, she pretended to be Mr. Slade inviting Mrs. Ansley to meet him for a romantic interlude at the Colosseum. Now, many years later, Mrs. Slade confesses to her friend that the letter was really a fake. Mrs. Anslcy, in turn, confesses that she sent Mr. Slade a letter in reply. And that they did indeed have that romantic meeting. Mrs. Slade is shocked but still feels superior because, she says, she had her husband during all those years of marriage. But Mrs. Ansley replies that she has had her lively daughter. Who's really Mr. Slade's biological daughter—the result of that one romantic fling. Eileen can't decide which woman is the winner.

CHAPTER 2
MAKING A POINT

Thesis Statements

A **thesis statement** is a sentence that explains the main purpose of an essay. It can be just a short, simple sentence stating an opinion or attitude, or it may divide the main idea into two, three, or four parts. A thesis statement has to be broad enough to cover everything contained in the essay but specific enough to explain your purpose.

Simple Thesis Statement:

If you are ready for it, an online course can be a good choice.

Developed Thesis Statement:

If you are ready for the extra work and have the necessary self-discipline, an online course will provide a different, and in some ways richer, experience than you can have in a classroom.

Although a simple thesis statement is often satisfactory, a developed one provides a map for the rest of the essay and thus guides the reader more. As a reader, which of the two thesis statements above gives you a clearer idea of what to expect in the essay? The developed thesis statement tells us that the writer will discuss the amount of work in an online course, the self-discipline needed to keep up with assignments, and the ways in which you can get

something out of distance learning that you cannot get in a classroom. It makes some specific promises to the reader. The simple
thesis statement leaves us less certain what to expect.

Thesis Statements Must Take a Position

A thesis statement must state the whole purpose of the essay. Why
would the following sentence not make a good thesis statement for
the sample essay?

> Online courses are now offered at ninety percent of American
> colleges.

This is a specific factual statement. It might make a good lead-
in to arouse interest, but it does not state an argument or explain
the purpose of the whole essay.

Thesis Statements Must Be Precise

Although thesis statements must be broad enough to state an
essay's main purpose, they should never be fuzzy or confusing.
Remember that catchall words such as _bad_, _good_, _nice_, _great_,
interesting, and _thing_ are not precise. What is good to one person
is bad to another; what one person finds interesting another finds
tedious. Try to find more precise key words for your thesis statements. Compare these two thesis statements:

> A. _Extraterrestrials on Campus_ is a bad film.
> B. _Extraterrestrials on Campus_ is a pointless, tasteless film with a
> predictable plot and outmoded cinematic techniques.

Sentence A doesn't guide the reader much. It says only that
the writer is going to make negative remarks about the film.
Sentence B states what kind of faults the writer is going to find
in the film.

TEST YOURSELF: THESIS STATEMENTS

Identify which sentence in each of the pairs below might make a
suitable thesis statement for an essay:

1. A. The damage from Hurricane Katrina to New Orleans was
   over $80 billion.

    B. Emergency response plans need to be improved in most large U.S. cities.

2. A. The Giants won the game 27 to 21.
    B. The game between the Giants and the Redskins was full of suspense and unexpected reversals.

3. A. The current prison system lacks adequate means for rehabilitation and psychiatric counseling.
    B. The state prison at Capital City contains 1400 inmates.

4. A. Levels of alcohol in the blood can be tested by instruments.
    B. Drunken driving can be controlled better by the use of technology than by new laws.

5. A. My vacation in Morocco was wonderful because I met some remarkable people and visited archaeological sites.
    B. I visited Morocco for two weeks in March.

6. A. Women's fashions this year reflect the 1980s but are very practical.
    B. New fashions for women are interesting.

7. A. Poe's "The Tell-Tale Heart" is a scary story.
    B. Poe's "The Tell-Tale Heart" reveals several features of a psychotic mind.

Answers: 1. B 2. B 3. A 4. B 5. A 6. A 7. B

Introductory Paragraphs

The first paragraph in an essay serves several purposes. Its main purpose is to let the reader know what the essay is about, usually in a thesis statement, and to arouse the reader's interest. Starting with the thesis statement in your first sentence, however, is usually too blunt. Usually it is better to lead up to the thesis statement in some way. Think of the three-step design as a useful pattern for your first paragraph: lead-in, tie-in, and thesis statement.

Starting with the Three-Step Design
Begin your paragraph with an effective **lead-in**. This attention-getter can be one of several types:

- A question
- A quotation or other amusing remark

- A short, thought-provoking statement
- A surprising fact or statistic
- A problem or riddle

After capturing the reader's interest with a creative lead-in, find a way to focus that interest on the subject. The two or three sentences in which you do this are your **tie-in**. Finally, move smoothly from your tie-in to your thesis statement. The three-step design—lead-in, tie-in, thesis statement—is not a universal formula, but it may help you begin essays effectively.

Model Introductory Paragraph

Taking a course online can be a rich experience, if you are ready for it. Because I was not quite prepared to change my study habits, my first distance learning course almost became a disaster. However, I was able to make some adjustments in my attitude and routine quickly enough to learn a lot in the course. From my experience, I would advise anyone planning to take a course online to keep several things in mind: Distance learning does not require you to be a computer scientist, but neither is it an easy way out of difficult courses. If you are ready for the extra work and have the self-discipline to do assignments regularly, an online course will be a different, and in some ways richer, experience than you can have in a classroom.

To create organized paragraphs like this, you may have to do some prewriting experiments to identify your main purpose and supporting details. You will probably write a rough draft of your introductory paragraph and revise it after you have composed the rest of your essay.

Avoid Bad Starts

Watch out for these common problems with introductions. These methods may be tempting to use, but they usually produce weak essays.

- Do not begin by apologizing:

  In this essay I am supposed to write about the effect of instructional technology. I never took a distance learning course and I don't have very good keyboard skills. All I can say is that online courses are very important for some people and are here to stay. Every time I look at the schedule of classes, I see whole lists of courses given online. Sometime maybe I will try to take one of them. I wish I knew more about technology.

This kind of introduction reads like a piece of focused writing in which the writer is searching for something to say about the topic. The paragraph has no organization, no lead-in, and no thesis statement. Do not tell the reader what you do not know; explore what you *do* know through prewriting techniques until you find a good way to begin.

- Do not bore your reader by mechanically previewing too much of your essay:

    I am going to discuss instructional technology in this essay. First, I plan to talk about how important distance learning is to some students who can't attend regular classroom courses. My next paragraph will be about how computers can be used in classrooms. Then I will discuss different kinds of courses that use technology. Finally, I will stress how important technology will be in higher education over the next decade.

This writer calls too much attention to her plan. No viewer at the beginning of a film wants to know the entire plot and all the cinematic and audio techniques used in making it. Be clear about your intentions, but do not bore the reader.

- Do not begin with grandiose statements that fail to lead into your thesis:

    Since the beginning of time human beings have invented new technological advances that have helped and hindered the progress of education toward perfection. In modern times of today, nothing has had a bigger impact on the way people learn than one single invention: a machine called the computer. This machine will be remembered as the greatest learning tool of all time.

This writer shows enthusiasm but needs to focus his ideas. *Show* rather than *tell* the reader what is important and exciting about your subject, and concentrate on a topic that is limited enough for you to discuss in depth.

TEST YOURSELF: INTRODUCTORY PARAGRAPHS

Read the three sample paragraphs that follow. Identify the one that is carefully organized; find the lead-in, tie-in, and thesis statement. Explain why the other two would fail as introductory paragraphs.

Paragraph A:

Poetry is one of the most wonderful things in the world. Since the beginning of history, people have written poems. There are many kinds of poems, long poems, and short poems. Everybody likes to read poems and most people like to write them. Without poetry, where would we be? Poetry is the best way to spend your time. If you read and write poems, you will be a better person. Poetry will be around until the end of time.

Paragraph B:

Can a poem written in conversational language express deep meaning? Robert Frost's poem "The Road Not Taken" reads like an ordinary person talking to us, but gives us wisdom to guide our lives. Its plain language allows the reader to concentrate on the details of the poem and to imagine being in the situation it presents: facing a choice between two roads, which really stand for the choices we face in life. In this essay I will explain how the conversational style of this poem enables the reader to find personal meaning in imagined experience.

Paragraph C:

In this essay I am going to talk about the topic of poetry. As a child I liked to read poetry. My sister used to read poetry to me before I could read. I don't know much about how to write about poetry, but it's always hard to get started writing about anything. I don't like poems that have big words I can't understand. The poems I like are simple, but they say a lot in ordinary language. I'm not going to write about technical stuff like rhyme schemes and what kind of accents there are in every line. Poetry is hard to write about.

Answer: Paragraph A makes grandiose, over-generalized statements and would not lead in well to an essay. Paragraph C apologizes for the writer's confusion and wanders in several directions. Paragraph B focuses on a specific poem and makes a clear point that could be developed in an essay.

WRITING TIP #2

In this age of instant messaging, readers are more impatient than ever. Because of this, some readers may not pay close attention to all parts of your essay. If they don't, you can guess which part they are most likely to notice: your introduction. Readers expect you to explain your main purpose near the beginning of your essay, so be sure not to disappoint them. Even better, make your opening so interesting that they will want to read your whole essay carefully. Be sure that your purpose is clear by the end of your first paragraph.

Writing Exercises: Basic, Intermediate, Challenge

☐ Basic Exercise: Thesis Statements

Identify which sentence in each pair would make a more effective thesis statement for an essay; explain what is defective in the other one.

1. A. On my trip to Las Vegas I lost $300.

   B. My trip to Las Vegas taught me two lessons: plan ahead, and don't gamble.

2. A. News magazines cover stories in more detail than television news.

   B. I like to read news magazines and watch television news.

3. A. Soccer is played in almost every country.

   B. There are three reasons why soccer is becoming more popular in American schools.

4. A. My sister's experience with three diets shows which one really works.

   B. My sister is really overweight and needs to go on a diet.

5. A. A lot of people shop online nowadays.

   B. Several tips will help you become a smarter online shopper.

6. A. To improve credibility, the Olympics needs improved judging and drug testing.

    B. The summer Olympics was held in Athens in 2004.

7. A. This essay will be about physical therapy.

    B. This essay will explain the education and training requirements for careers in physical therapy.

▣ Intermediate Exercise: Thesis Statements

Rewrite these sentences to make them more effective thesis statements:

Original sentence: Aiden's first year in college was a good experience.

Revised sentence: Aiden's first year in college changed him from an adolescent to an adult.

1. Ted has two brothers and three sisters.

2. The mall where I worked had thirty-six stores in it.

3. Reading novels takes a lot of time.

4. Biology 101 is a good course.

5. Tiger Woods is a famous golfer.

6. I like to watch reality television shows.

7. You see people talking on cell phones everywhere.

▣ Challenge Exercise: Thesis Statements

Write precise, developed thesis statements for imaginary essays on these topics:

1. Teenagers and their parents

   Thesis statement: _____

   _____

2. Marriage and divorce

   Thesis statement: _____

   _____

3. College courses
   Thesis statement: _____

   _____

4. Choosing careers
   Thesis statement: _____

   _____

5. Political campaigns
   Thesis statement: _____

   _____

6. A film you liked
   Thesis statement: _____

   _____

7. A book you have read
   Thesis statement _____

   _____

Proofreading Practice: Agreement of Subjects and Verbs

Watch Those *S*-Endings

Writing a thesis statement always involves matching a subject, either singular or plural, with an action. As in all sentences, the verb in a thesis sentence must agree in number with the subject. Most errors in subject-verb agreement involve missing *s*-endings on nouns or verbs. Sometimes writers put *s*-endings where they should not be.

Typical errors in thesis statements:

Incorrect singular statement:	Technology <u>help</u> students become active learners.
Corrected form:	Technology <u>helps</u> students become active learners.
Incorrect plural statement:	Technological innovations <u>helps</u> students become active learners.
Corrected form:	Technological innovations <u>help</u> students become active learners.

Remember the **one-*s* pattern**: In most sentences, either the verb has the *s*-ending (singular) or the noun subject has the *s*-ending (plural):

Singular: An outstanding student <u>submits</u> work on time.

Plural: Outstanding <u>students</u> submit work on time.

TEST YOURSELF: SUBJECT-VERB AGREEMENT

Find the errors in *s*-endings in these sentences. Add *s*-endings where they are missing and eliminate *s*-endings where they do not belong. One sentence is correct.

1. Sarah's cousin like Sarah's new hairstyle.
2. Three players wants to join another team.
3. Some candidates refuses to accept public funds.
4. The spring vacation this year begins on Tuesday.
5. Most essays needs strong introductory paragraphs.
6. The professor always assign a long reading over the weekend.
7. Cars with ample interior space sells well.

Answers: 1. likes 2. want 3. refuse 4. correct 5. need 6. assigns 7. sell

---

Proofreading Exercises: Basic, Intermediate, Challenge

☐ Basic Exercise: Subject-Verb Agreement

Find the seven errors in the following passage. Rewrite the paragraph with corrections:

> Shirley plans her weekdays in three stages. She usually spend her whole morning in college classes. She always take notes and participates in discussions. At one o'clock she always feel tired and hungry, so she heads for the cafeteria. That is where she meets her friends Jennifer and Jonathan. They both live in town and commutes to campus. In the afternoon, from 2:00 until 6:00, her job in the law school library take up all of her time. After work, she relax and has a light dinner. Then in the evening she and her friends often goes to parties, discos, or movies. Her schedule keeps her active and socially busy, and she needs the weekend to rest and do homework.

▣ Intermediate Exercise: Subject-Verb Agreement

Find the seven errors in the following passage. Rewrite the paragraph with corrections:

> Wise investing depend upon several factors. It involves your income, needs, and willingness to take risks. Some people invests their money only in stocks. Other opportunities also exists. Municipal bonds, mutual funds, and term savings accounts all offers investment advantages. The right kind of investment for you mean considering several elements. Tax benefits from municipal bonds appeals to some investors. Stocks present possibilities for high income but with high risk. The investor who wants to avoid risks often choose Mutual funds. Corporate bonds also offer high income possibilities but also with greater risk than municipal bonds.

▣ Challenge Exercise: Subject-Verb Agreement

Find the seven errors in the following passage. Rewrite the paragraph with corrections:

> Some expert believe that one of the chief problems in American education is the inability of student to understand and evaluate knowledge. Howard Gardner, a professor of education at Harvard University, in a book called *The Unschooled Mind*, write that too many students think according to stereotypes. In the social sciences, for example, they bring to the study of a problem their assumptions about human nature based on their own experience. In the arts, they often retains tastes acquired in childhood and nourished by popular culture and do not acquire more complex and subtle ways of appreciating music, art, and literature. When they analyze a historical event or evaluate a poem or piece of music, too many students rely on their habitual responses, which derives from a narrow range of biases and preconceptions. Therefore a major challenge of education is to help students develop the power to analyze, evaluate, and appreciate new problems, situations, and experiences by drawing on a deep understanding of academic disciplines. Although acquiring factual knowledge is part of learning, memorization of information do not guarantee that students understands the meaning and value of the factual knowledge they have acquired.

CHAPTER 3
DEVELOPING YOUR BODY PARAGRAPHS AND MAKING CONCLUSIONS

Explaining and Illustrating Ideas in Body Paragraphs

The most common problem with many writers' first drafts is lack of development. Think of development as explaining and illustrating ideas, not just adding words. Even writers with a fluent command of English and smart ideas may fail to say enough about the topic they discuss. There is no way of getting around it: explaining and illustrating your ideas takes work. There are techniques to help you develop your ideas, but no quick and easy ones. Development requires thinking, composing, and revising.

Applying Techniques of Development

You will find it easier to develop ideas if you acquire a variety of development methods. One approach is to **analyze** and **explain** your topic. If your subject has complicated and controversial aspects, do not rush over this part of the essay. Explain the complexities and controversies; go into detail in explaining your point. Another technique is to give **examples**, either from **personal experience** or **general knowledge** acquired from the news media and your reading. A third is to **draw analogies** by comparing your subject to some parallel thing or concept. You may want to **acknowledge your reader's viewpoint** if it is likely that many people will disagree with you or have a different perspective on the topic. In most of the best writing, there is some **appeal to emotions** as well, which can be done through your style, the examples you choose, or the way in which your writing strikes a responsive chord in the reader's feelings.

In research essays, you will use **published sources of information**, such as books, articles, and Web sites. Beware the "data dump," however. It is tempting to take whole patches of words from a Web source and paste them into your essay without thinking carefully. If you want to use material from printed or Web sources, as you're often expected to do in college essays, read them carefully and evaluate their content. Passing along whole blocks of writing from another source may give you a sense of power, but it will not impress a reader unless you select the information carefully and present it effectively to fulfill the purpose of your essay.

Below are some examples of techniques of development used by writers.

Analyzing a Topic

Here is one student's analysis of an issue in education:

> There are many reasons why students with good abilities do poorly in school and college. Sometimes they have personal problems that hold them back, causing them to undermine their own progress. Their peers, especially ones who have a negative attitude toward school, may influence them. Some students believe that it is more important to earn money than to earn a diploma or college degree. They may put off completing their education so they can buy the clothes, jewelry, and electronic equipment they want. Other students have learning disabilities and, even though they are very intelligent, may not get the special help they need to succeed in school. Finally, many students attend schools in which the instruction is not in their native language. They may take a number of years to catch up to native speakers and not reach their full potential right away.

Remember to use your powers of critical thinking to explore and analyze the range of your topic. Brainstorming, focused writing, or cubing may help you recognize the many aspects of your topic.

Using Personal Experience

Here is a passage in which the writer draws on personal experience to make a point about the power books exercise in the minds of children. Mike Rose explains how reading and writing were connected in his youth as he told stories to his friends in the street:

> Reading opened up the world. There I was, a skinny bookworm drawing the attention of street kids who, in any other circumstances, would have had me for breakfast. Like an epic tale-teller, I developed the stories as I went along, relying on a flexible plot line and repository of heroic events. I had a great time. I sketched out trajectories with my finger on Frank's dusty truck bed. And I stretched out each story's climax, creating cliff-hangers like the ones I saw in the Saturday serials. These stories created for me a temporary community.
>
> —Mike Rose, *Lives on the Boundary* (New York: Penguin, 1989): 21

Mike Rose's book is mostly about his own life, so naturally he writes about personal experience. In some college essays, however, it is unusual to write about personal matters. If you are not sure what to do on a specific assignment, discuss it with your instructor.

Using Analogies

Here is a famous passage from Shakespeare's play *As You Like It* in which a character named Jacques develops an idea by comparing life to a theater. Notice how each detail helps to develop the thought:

> All the world's a stage,
> And all the men and women merely players.
> They have their exits and their entrances,
> And one man in his time plays many parts,
> His acts being seven ages. At first the infant,
> Mewling and puking in the nurse's arms.   *mewling* meowing
> Then the whining schoolboy, with his satchel   like a cat
> And shining morning face, creeping like snail
> Unwillingly to school. And then the lover,
> Sighing like furnace, with a woeful ballad   *bearded like the*
> Made to his mistress' eyebrow. Then a soldier,   *pard* with whiskers
> Full of strange oaths and bearded like the pard,   like a leopard

Jealous in honor, sudden, and quick in quarrel,
Seeking the bubble reputation
Even in the cannon's mouth. And then the justice,
In fair round belly with good capon lined,   *capon lined* fat
With eyes severe and beard of formal cut,   from eating chicken
Full of wise saws and modern instances;   *saws* sayings
And so he plays his part. The sixth age shifts
Into the lean and slippered pantaloon,
With spectacles on nose and pouch on side,
His youthful hose, well saved, a world too wide
For his shrunk shank; and his big manly voice,   *shrunk shank*
Turning again toward childish treble, pipes   skinny legs
And whistles in his sound. Last scene of all,
That ends this strange, eventful history,   *mere oblivion*
Is second childishness and mere oblivion,   nothingness
Sans teeth, sans eyes, sans taste, sans everything.   *sans* without

—William Shakespeare. From *As You Like It*, Act 2, Scene 7, lines 138–165.

Comparisons of this kind can help us understand a topic better, but remember that an analogy is *only* a comparison and therefore doesn't by itself prove very much about the original subject.

Acknowledging the Reader

Below is a passage from the famous "Letter from Birmingham Jail" by Dr. Martin Luther King, Jr. Notice how he begins his letter by recognizing the objections of the clergymen to whom the letter is addressed and appealing to their religious convictions:

April 16, 1963

MY DEAR FELLOW CLERGYMEN:
    While confined here in the Birmingham city jail, I came across your recent statement calling my present activities "unwise and untimely." Seldom do I pause to answer criticism of my work and ideas. If I sought to answer all the criticisms that cross my desk, my secretaries would have little time for anything other than such correspondence in the course of the day, and I would have no time for constructive work. But since I feel that you are men of genuine good will and that your criticisms are sincerely set forth, I want to try to answer your statements in what I hope will be patient and reasonable terms.

I think I should indicate why I am here in Birmingham, since you have been influenced by the view which argues against "outsiders coming in." I have the honor of serving as president of the Southern Christian Leadership Conference, an organization operating in every southern state, with headquarters in Atlanta, Georgia. We have some eighty-five affiliated organizations across the South, and one of them is the Alabama Christian Movement for Human Rights. Frequently we share staff, educational and financial resources with our affiliates. Several months ago the affiliate here in Birmingham asked us to be on call to engage in a nonviolent direct-action program if such were deemed necessary. We readily consented, and when the hour came we lived up to our promise. So I, along with several members of my staff, am here because I was invited here. I am here because I have organizational ties here.

But more basically, I am in Birmingham because injustice is here. Just as the prophets of the eighth century B.C. left their villages and carried their "thus saith the Lord" far beyond the boundaries of their home towns, and just as the Apostle Paul left his village of Tarsus and carried the gospel of Jesus Christ to the far corners of the Greco-Roman world, so am I compelled to carry the gospel of freedom beyond my own home town. Like Paul, I must constantly respond to the Macedonian call for aid.

Moreover, I am cognizant of the interrelatedness of all communities and states. I cannot sit idly by in Atlanta and not be concerned about what happens in Birmingham. Injustice anywhere is a threat to justice everywhere. We are caught in an inescapable network of mutuality, tied in a single garment of destiny. Whatever affects one directly, affects all indirectly. Never again can we afford to live with the narrow, provincial "outside agitator" idea. Anyone who lives inside the United States can never be considered an outsider anywhere within its bounds. . . .

—Martin Luther King Jr. Excerpt from "Letter from Birmingham Jail"

Dr. King then goes on to explain why his nonviolent campaign against racial segregation is necessary and right. Before making his argument, however, he captures the attention and sympathies of his readers by talking directly to them and understanding their point of view, even though he disagrees with it. By basing his argument on their shared principles, he can more effectively persuade them that his cause is just.

Appealing to Emotion

In the case of Alzheimer's disease, it is rarely the patient who recognizes the need for company in the journey through travail. But there is probably no disability of our time in which the presence of support groups can help so decisively to ensure the emotional survival of the closest witnesses to the disintegration. . . . There is strength in numbers, even when the numbers are only one or two understanding people who can soften the anguish by the simple act of listening.

That anguish consists of many parts, and some of them cannot be dealt with unless with a sympathetic and knowing listener. Is it possible that the burden of this disease does not become a source of resentment and sometimes repugnance to everyone it drags along in its loathsome wake? Can anyone maim a great piece of his or her life without seething? Is there a single person who can forbearingly watch as the object of his or her brightest love involutes into incomprehension and decay?

—Sherwin B. Nuland, *How We Die: Reflections on Life's Final Chapter*
(New York: Knopf, 1994): 106

In this passage, Dr. Nuland, in the midst of giving a scientific explanation of Alzheimer's disease, appeals to the reader's emotions to convey how devastating the disease can be on families. See how many emotions you can identify in his discussion.

Using Public Sources of Information

One task you are certain to be assigned in college courses is to use researched materials from the Web or the library to back up the arguments in your papers. This research can be done for any subject. Below is a brief example of how to use a source to make a point about a short story:

In Alice Walker's short story, "Everyday Use," patchwork quilts serve as a central symbol as well as the subject of a family quarrel. Over the centuries quilts acquired symbolic importance in African American culture. According to Houston Baker and Charlotte Pierce-Baker, quilts "crafted from bits of worn overalls, shredded uniforms, tattered petticoats, and outgrown dresses" came to represent the "patterned wholeness in the African diaspora" (309). Walker incorporates this traditional symbolism for the purpose of revealing the strength as well as the inner tensions of African American families. She also causes the reader to think about the meaning of the word *heritage*.

Notice that when you use sources this way, you must fit the quotations into your sentences grammatically, put them in quotation marks, and refer to the sources in parentheses (usually with the author's name and page, but in this case the authors are already mentioned). At the end of the paper, you must create a bibliography, or list of sources. The source referred to above would look like this on your list:

Baker, Houston A., Jr., and Charlotte Pierce-Baker. "Patches: Quilts and Community in Alice Walker's 'Everyday Use.'" In *Alice Walker: Critical Perspectives Past and Present*. Ed. Henry Louis Gates, Jr. and K. A. Appiah. New York: Amistad Press, 1993, 309–316.

For a complete lesson on using research materials, see Chapter 14.

Choosing Modes of Development

Writing is often classified into categories called **rhetorical modes**. The **narrative** mode is storytelling, whether fiction or nonfiction. The **descriptive** mode refers to writing that paints a word portrait of a person, place, or institution. There are several kinds of **expository** modes, such as **process analysis**, **enumeration**, **definition**, and **classification**. **Comparison and contrast** is a writing mode often used in academic work, and **persuasion**, also called **argumentation**, is a familiar form of writing in editorials and political writing.

These categories identify the purpose of the essay and the method by which it is structured. Most essays fit loosely into one of these types, but these categories are not completely separate, like biological species. A single essay usually draws on several of these modes and combines them for a total effect. For practice, however, it is useful to group essays into these modes to explore varied kinds of writing.

Some college writing assignments require a particular mode. In other cases, you may have some choice, such as an assignment that requires an expository presentation but does not specify exactly how you should arrange and develop it. Being familiar with the different modes and choosing the one that will be most effective is a key to successful writing. It is also important to familiarize yourself with the best techniques to use in different modes, as well as some of the problems they may present, both as writing strategies and as grammatical challenges.

WRITING TIP #3

Students often ask their instructors how long an assignment should be, as if the only goal in completing an assignment were writing a lot of words. If you think of your essay as a 750-word hike, you will probably head into the writing process with blinders on, counting your words but ignoring many of the ways you could enliven your topic. Instead, try creating a different mental picture of your project before you write—see it, perhaps, not as a journey but as an empty canvas to be filled with colors and shapes, a meal to be prepared with varied ingredients, or a garden to be planted with many flowers and vegetables. Imagining such nonlinear tasks may help you think in terms of variety, richness, and the interrelation of parts. Your finished essay will of course take the reader on a journey from beginning to end, but while you are creating the essay, it is better not to make a beeline for your last paragraph, counting words as you go. Be resourceful about adding material to your composition anywhere—at the beginning, in the middle, or at the end.

Concluding Paragraphs

Concluding paragraphs should look in two directions—backward to sum up what you've said, and forward to suggest further thought. Like introductory paragraphs, they are usually short. Your concluding statements should leave the reader with a sense of completeness and a desire to think more about the subject. Like the opening, the ending of your essay should be dramatic, witty, imaginative, amusing, or thought-provoking. It might pose a question, a prediction, or a paradox. It should remind the reader of something you said at the beginning of the essay, but it should not merely repeat words from the first paragraph. Think of the concluding paragraph as an upside-down version of the introductory paragraph. It may begin by reemphasizing the main idea (but not by restating the thesis sentence word for word) and end with statements that wrap up the discussion with humor, emotional appeal, or insight.

Conclusions to Avoid

- **Do not introduce important ideas that are not supported in your essay.** If you try to complete your essay in one hasty draft, your "concluding" paragraph may be the one in which you discover important new ideas. If this happens, either rethink the whole essay, using material from this "concluding" section as the main point expressed near the beginning of your essay, or rethink the concluding paragraph to make it fit the essay you have written.

    Consider this attempt at a conclusion to our imaginary essay on distance learning:

    > So we can see that technology has become very important in higher education. In fact, businesses and government agencies use technology just as much as colleges do. Try to imagine banks without ATMs, transit systems without computer programs, and police departments without cellular phones and data files. Technology has changed every part of our lives today.

    This paragraph jumps off the track. The essay is about online courses, but at the end the writer suddenly becomes interested in other uses of computer technology. The concluding paragraph is a bad place to change your topic, just when you should be stressing the points already made.

- **Do not end with a detailed, monotonous summary.** Another kind of conclusion that does not succeed in a short essay is the mechanical summary. Sometimes a very long piece of writing, such as a book or dissertation, especially if it is complicated, needs a summary to help the reader digest and remember the points made in it. In a short college essay, however, such a summary is a great way to bore the reader. Consider this paragraph as an ending to our essay on computers in higher education:

> In summary, I have discussed in this essay some of the ways that computers make higher education more efficient. The first advantage I discussed was taking courses at home. In the next paragraph I talked about asynchronous discussions in online courses. Then I explained the advantages of having access to professors through e-mail. When you have read what I explained about these advantages, you will understand why it is important to take more courses online.

This paragraph emphasizes the writer's plan when the focus should be on the topic itself. Give the reader a sense of order, and make some indirect reference to your opening, but do not overdo the repetition.

• **Do not fade at the end.** Often when you have put a lot of effort into writing an essay, you may be tired and not want to put much effort into your final paragraph. Remember that some readers will look to your conclusion for a concise, forceful statement of your purpose and expect it to be some of your best writing in the essay. Do not disappoint them.

Model Concluding Paragraph

Here is a more successful concluding paragraph for our essay:

> Online courses, as I discovered, can be exciting because of the features you can not experience in a classroom. In threaded discussions you can see what everyone else is thinking, and the remarks are saved, unlike a class discussion, where many students remain silent and no record is kept. You also receive more feedback from both the instructor and your classmates than you are likely to get in a traditional class. Materials from Web sites make the course richer as well. If you are ready for the extra work and have the self-discipline to keep up with the assignments, these advantages of distance education are for you.

Note that the writer makes an indirect reference to the advice given in the model introductory paragraph above, that students should be realistic about the demands of online courses. This link to the introduction creates a sense of completeness.

Writing Exercises: Basic, Intermediate, Challenge

☐ Basic Exercise: Using Personal Experience

Begin a paragraph with the sentence provided below. Develop the idea with at least six additional sentences, using **personal experience** as a method of development.

> An important change in my life taught me a lesson about myself.

▣ Intermediate Exercise: Using an Analogy

Begin a paragraph with the sentence provided below. Develop the idea with at least six additional sentences, expanding your **analogy** as a method of development.

> My family is just like a _____ (fill in the blank with a word such as team, circus, sitcom, soap opera, corporation, etc.).

▣ Challenge Exercise: Acknowledging Your Reader

Begin a paragraph with the sentence provided below. Develop the idea with at least six additional sentences, **acknowledging your reader's viewpoint** as a method of development. Explain why others believe what they do and why you think they are mistaken.

> Many people believe that making a lot of money is the most important goal in life.

Proofreading Practice: Special Problems with Agreement

While developing your thesis, you should write sentences that are varied and interesting. Varying sentence styles, however, requires careful matching of subjects and verbs. This is a good time to review this aspect of grammar because not all of your sentences will follow a simple pattern of subject-verb-object and there are some special problems with agreement.

Forms of *Be, Have,* and *Do*

The common helping verbs **be**, **have**, and **do** present special difficulties with agreement because they have more forms than other verbs. Instead of just adding an *s*-ending, *be* has these forms:

	Singular	**Plural**
First person:	I <u>am</u>	We <u>are</u>
Second person:	You <u>are</u>	You <u>are</u>
Third person:	He, she, it <u>is</u>	They <u>are</u>

Note: In the **past tense**, *be* is the only verb that can cause agreement problems because it has two forms:

She <u>was</u>   They <u>were</u>

Have has two forms in the present: *has* for third person singular and *have* for all other subjects.

He <u>has</u>   They <u>have</u>

Do also has two forms: *does* for third person singular and *do* for all the others. Be careful about *don't* and *doesn't* as well.

She <u>does</u>   They <u>do</u>
She <u>doesn't</u>   They <u>don't</u>

Test Yourself: Be, Have, and Do

Tell whether the forms of *be, have,* and *do* are correct; if not, supply the correct forms:

1. Students who doesn't join the program will lose out.
2. Raul thinks he have the best chance to win.
3. One of the old highways are going to be resurfaced.
4. Not all of the banks does business on Saturday.
5. Margaret always has a positive attitude.

6. Every workshop in the lab are going to last one hour.

7. Some of my friends does their shopping on the Web.

Answers: 1. don't 2. has 3. is 4. do 5. correct 6. is 7. do

Subjects That Come After Verbs

You may have difficulty with sentences that do not follow the ordinary subject-verb-object order. When a verb comes before the subject, you have to match the verb with the subject that appears later in the sentence.

Verbs come before subjects in several kinds of sentences:

1. Questions containing reversed word order:

   v   s
   Are there any new <u>workers</u> here today?

   v   s
   Where **have** the <u>clinics</u> been established?

2. Sentences beginning with *there* or *here* place the verb before the subject:

   v   s
   There **have** been several <u>problems</u> with that model.

   v   s
   Here **is** a beautiful <u>photograph</u> of Hilary as a teenager.

3. Sentences beginning with descriptive phrases sometimes place the verb before the subject:

   v   s
   Behind the gate **were** three armed <u>guards</u>.

   v   s
   Projected on both screens **was** a clever <u>icon</u>.

Notice that in such sentences you should not try to match the verb with the word right before it so that the combination sounds right. You must find the subject *after* the verb. In the last sentence, not the *screens were* but the *icon was* projected on the screens.

TEST YOURSELF: SUBJECTS THAT COME AFTER VERBS

Tell whether the verb forms are correct; if not, supply the correct forms:

1. There isn't many ways to get to the airport.

2. Why have Shirley registered for both courses?

3. On the back of the computer was two USB ports.

4. What was the vice president and his advisors thinking?

5. Here is a good example of special treatment for visitors.

6. Among the first deliveries was some suits and dresses from Italy.

7. Where does the atmosphere end and outer space begin?

Answers: 1. aren't 2. has 3. were 4. were 5. correct 6. were 7. correct

Special Subjects

Some subjects are hard to match with verbs because they seem to be plural but are singular grammatically or because they are singular when used one way and plural when used another.

Singular Pronouns	Singular/Plural Words
everyone	all
anyone	half
someone	some
everybody	most
anybody	more
somebody	

Write *everyone has* some kind of special talent, not *have*. *Each*, *either*, and *one* are also singular, even though they are often followed by plural phrases. *Each* of the students *is* (not *are*). *Either* of the women *has* the right to participate (not *have*).

Some words are singular when they refer to amounts and plural when they refer to numbers.

<u>All</u> of the money **has** been deposited (singular—an amount).

<u>All</u> of the employees **are** required to wear passes (plural—a number).

Group Nouns

Nouns that refer to groups of people present a special problem: Words such as *army, family, team, jury, chorus, union, committee, company*, and *organization* seem to be plural because they refer to many people;

however, they have plural forms (*armies, families,* etc.), so the singular forms should be used with singular verbs. An *army invades* another country, or the *team has* a winning season. When you refer to such words as single units, using the singular form, use singular verbs as well. However, when you use the word to refer to the individual members of the group, it is permissible to use a plural verb. Some writers find it awkward and consider it incorrect to write the *team are* taking their places on the field. It is less objectionable to write "the *players are* taking their places," or "the *members* of the team *are* taking their places." Just be sure to tell the difference between the group as a unit (singular) and separate individuals (plural).

Verbs Separated from Subjects
by Prepositional Phrases

A verb will often be separated from its subject by a prepositional phrase. Do not be confused by such phrases. *A subject cannot be part of a prepositional phrase.* If you try to match the verb with a word next to it, you may miss the subject and choose the wrong verb form. Notice the difference:

   s   v
1. The <u>musicians</u> **are** busy rehearsing.

   s   v
2. <u>One</u> of the musicians **is** not here yet.

In sentence 2, the subject *one* is separated from the verb *is* by a prepositional phrase, "of the musicians." You must mentally cross out the phrase and match the subject with the verb: "<u>One</u> . . . **is** not here yet." What are prepositional phrases? They are phrases made out of the little relational words like *in, of, with,* etc. Problems with agreement occur most often with sentences beginning "One of the . . ." Remember that the word *one* requires you to use a singular verb form: "<u>One</u> of my favorite films **is** *Shrek.*"

TEST YOURSELF: GROUP NOUNS AND SPECIAL SUBJECTS

Determine whether the verb forms are correct; if not, supply the correct forms:

1. One of the best ways to buy groceries are to join a food cooperative.

2. Everybody has to take at least one distance learning course.

3. The committee are scheduled to meet every Wednesday afternoon.

4. One of the smartest students never talk in class.

5. All of the income from the album go to charities.

6. Someone has to volunteer to be secretary.

7. The noise of the trucks and buses always drown out conversation.

Answers: 1. is 2. correct 3. is 4. talks 5. goes 6. correct 7. drowns

Proofreading Exercises: Basic, Intermediate, Challenge

☐ Basic Exercise: Special Problems with Agreement

Find the seven errors in the following passage. Rewrite the paragraph with corrections:

Everybody in Steven's family have a nickname. Most of them has names associated with their personal features. His brother Wade, for instance, is heavyset so they call him Wide. His cousin Larry, who is tall, is called Lofty, and his female cousin Kathy, who is always busy at her computer, is called Keys. Some of the others has been given names that are the opposite of their traits. For example, one of his sisters have been nicknamed Skinhead because she has beautiful long hair. The family have named Uncle Manuel, who is unusually aggressive, Mouse, and his sister Serene, who is very quiet, Siren. Among all these nicknames are one that Steven is not sure about—his own. His cousins all call him Star, but he doesn't know whether it is a term of admiration or a joke. He hopes that all of his family members thinks he really is outstanding, but he suspects they may be making fun of him.

▥ Intermediate Exercise: Special Problems with Agreement

Find the seven errors in the following passage. Rewrite the paragraph with corrections:

Many people likes to communicate by e-mail rather than writing letters or talking on the telephone. One of the reasons are that it is much faster than sending a letter. Another reason is that when you send an e-mail message, the other person don't have to be there at the other end. Almost everyone leave telephone messages too, but on the telephone you don't have time to compose a message, and voice messages has to be short. Among the other advantages of e-mail are the fact that you can send attachments of all sizes. Best of all have to be the cost; you don't have to buy stamps or pay for long-distance calls, even when you are communicating with a friend in another part of the country.

■ Challenge Exercise: Special Problems with Agreement

Find the seven errors in the following passage. Rewrite the paragraph with corrections:

American democracy is sometimes called the worst system of government, except for all the others. Among its most problematic features are the electoral system. Instead of voting directly for President and Vice President, American voters actually choose statewide electors, who casts all their votes for the candidate whose party wins the most votes in that state. And that candidate then gets all the electoral votes of that state, even when the total votes in that state is almost equal. Many voters then feel that their votes doesn't really count. In addition, during the campaign, the candidates tends to ignore the states that they are sure to win or lose and concentrate on the so-called "swing states," where their speeches and television appearances makes a big difference. And when a candidate wins the popular vote but lose the election because of the electoral count, as in the year 2000, there is sure to be much anger and resentment.

CHAPTER 4
GLOBAL REVISING: DOING AN EXTREME MAKEOVER

Like most college writers, you may find that your biggest chore is developing your thesis effectively and adequately. When you have done that, you will probably feel that your work is nearly finished. However, there is more to revision than just adding material, correcting a few errors, and transferring your essay from handwriting to the keyboard. The real revision begins after you have a complete and well-developed draft. The difference between an acceptable but unexciting essay and a superior one (which often means the difference between and a B and an A) lies in the process of making changes in your thinking and wording.

Moving from a Draft to an Essay: A Glimpse of a Student Writer at Work

You have read Sarah Chen's essay, "Why Liberal Arts?" in its final form. Before reaching that final draft, however, Sarah did a lot of work thinking about the subject, as you saw in the section on prewriting activities. After doing some focused writing and clustering, she created a rough draft based on her outline. Read the draft below and notice the comments afterward, which were made by Sarah's instructor and helped her produce the final essay that you read in the introduction.

Liberal Arts in the Modern World

A good education is one of the most important things for anybody in this day and age. Most people say that you need a good education to survive but they don't think about what it means to get a good education. Is it really necessary nowadays to get a broad education?

Is making money the only thing? Our sociology teacher asked us which we would choose—a good education without a degree or a degree without an education. But some students don't think into the future. They forget that the job they are training for could become outdated, and then where are they? They don't have a good education to fall back on. People who have a broad education are better in other ways, too. They participate in society more intelligently than uneducated people, and they make better parents and family members in general.

It is also important for an individual to lead a happy life by being creative. Some people who have a good education do this on their jobs, and sometimes they take up hobbies that allow them to express their creativity in other ways. There is no doubt that making money by getting job training in business or computers is what many students want, but it may be more important to become a better educated human being while you can as a college student.

Most students major in business, accounting, engineering or some other major which will get them ready for a high-paying job. They think that the only thing that matters is making money. Maybe a liberal arts education is a better preparation for jobs than they realize.

If you recall from the section on prewriting, Sarah developed an outline for her draft. It looked like this:

Thesis: A liberal arts education is more important than ever in today's world.

I. People with liberal arts education contribute to society.

II. A liberal arts education enriches family life.

III. A liberal arts education makes an individual happier and more creative.

IV. Liberal arts is a good preparation for many careers.

Sarah's instructor praised her for following the outline but made some suggestions.

- First, the draft is very short and needs more development of each section.

- Each of the four points in the outline should be developed into a full separate paragraph, not squeezed together and left without enough explanation.

- Maybe the last topic about career preparation should come first, and that would leave the point about individual happiness as an effective closer. What do you think?

- The introduction should be more focused and interesting: maybe the story about the sociology class would make a good introduction.

- The conclusion should be separate from point number four about creativity; it should wrap up the entire essay.

Sarah decided that she needed to make her essay much longer and rethink her outline. She decided to change her introduction and to put the first topic of her outline last. As writers usually do when they make global revisions, she made major rearrangements in her plan and added a lot of material. Now go back and read the her essay on page 3 and see how much planning and revision went into producing her well-organized final draft.

Sarah also made some wording and grammar corrections in the draft, but these have been left out to emphasize what revision really is—re-visioning your work, looking at it again, and doing a makeover. You've seen people on television whose appearance is transformed in astonishing ways by experts at extreme makeovers. Always try to do the same with your early drafts and make the final version better written, better organized, and better developed.

Testing Your Thesis: Looking for Digressions and Weak Spots

When you examine your draft, first look at your main point, your thesis. Do not be afraid that the essay will collapse if you question your thesis. Read your essay as if you were a stranger who hasn't seen it before and disagrees with what you say. You can almost always make your point sharper and stronger by paying attention to how others respond to it.

What does it mean to test your thesis? Challenge it; give it the "Oh, yeah?" treatment. Let's say you are arguing in favor of lowering tuition at your college. That's a point that other students will usually agree with. But what would the college administration say? Think about why tuition is so high at most colleges. What costs are involved? Do you propose a way to bring down the costs? Should students do without something to reduce tuition? Should the college find other ways to bring in money? These are thoughts that you should explore in your essay. It is not enough just to take a position; you must consider the ways in which your ideas are necessarily connected to facts in the real world. Doing that will make your essay stronger and more credible.

Achieving Continuity through Transitions

Read your draft through to see whether it moves logically and smoothly from beginning to end. Does every sentence flow naturally from the one before? In the process of rethinking your work, you may leave out some necessary explanations between statements or between paragraphs. You may have written sentences that seem to contradict each other, and you may have made statements that are downright confusing. One general rule is that the reader cannot read your mind, only what you write on the page. Did you ever remark, "What the writer is trying to say is. . . ?" As a writer, you must actually say what you mean and not make the reader guess what you are *trying* to say.

For practice, begin reading a page from a book, preferably non-fiction, written by a professional writer whom you especially like. Read a few sentences slowly, then stop, covering up what comes next. Try to figure out what the writer will say next. Do this several times, noticing how carefully he or she moves from one thought to the next. Make a conscious effort to do this in your writing as well.

Improving Your Style: Breaking Up, Varying, and Combining Sentences

Read your work carefully aloud, noticing the rhythm of your sentences. Are they varied: some short, some long, and many in between? Do they have a natural flow, like good conversation? Be watchful for a tendency to write repetitively in short sentences that always begin with the subject followed by the verb. That habit will create an impression of immaturity. The opposite habit, of launching into meandering, shapeless sentences connected by *and* or *which*, will create the impression that you aren't sure what you want to say and haven't organized your thoughts.

Interacting with Your Reader (Reading Aloud to Others)

One of the best ways to benefit from the revision process is to have classmates read the draft of your essay and give their opinions. If they argue with you about the points you make, so much the better. Probably you will find that some readers agree and others disagree. That will complicate your process of revision but not weaken it. You have to decide how to deal with the objections raised by those who disagree and how to incorporate supporting points made by those who agree.

Some writers do not want others to read their drafts, at least not until they're finished with their final revisions. One reason may be that these writers believe that getting help from other students is cheating. On the contrary—this kind of help, which is often called feedback, is not only not cheating, it is one of the best ways to improve your work. No matter how many classmates' opinions you listen to, you have the final responsibility for the ideas you put forward in your essay and the facts and arguments you use to support them. Cheating would be having someone else write the essay for you.

You may feel shy about reading your work to others. This is understandable, especially with an early draft, which probably contains some writing errors and questionable statements. If you are working with other students whose early drafts are also incomplete, try to avoid grading or being judgmental. If you work in a group, think of it as an editorial staff, as if your essays were articles to be published in a magazine, and you want to make all of them as readable and convincing as possible.

PEER REVIEW QUESTIONS

In order to give responses that help you and your classmates improve the drafts of your essays, be sure to include comments on the items in the following checklist:

1. Here is my impression of what you say in your essay (write a summary in four or five sentences):

2. Your introduction is interesting. ☐ yes ☐ no
   Your introduction makes your main purpose clear.
   ☐ yes ☐ no
   The sentence that most nearly states your main purpose is the following:

3. You develop your main point well. ☐ yes ☐ no

4. Your method of developing ideas is the following:

5. Your conclusion (is/is not) effective for the following reason:

6. What I like best about your essay is the following:

7. I recommend you make the following changes:

WRITING TIP #4

Correcting one sentence problem can create the opposite problem. Breaking up run-together and stringy sentences can produce a choppy, immature style. Combining choppy sentences, unless you do it effectively, can result in sprawling, run-on sentences. The answer? Mastering sentence grammar and revising carefully. If you write too many stringy sentences, learn to break them up without producing fragments. If you write only short, simple sentences, practicing **subordination** will help you write in a more mature style.

Writing Exercises: Basic, Intermediate, Challenge

☐ **Basic Exercise: Achieving Continuity**

Complete the paragraph below, beginning with the sentence already written. Write at least five more sentences and end with the one already written. Try to make every sentence in the passage follow from the one before.

> When I get up in the morning, I go through a number of steps to get ready for work or classes. . . . When I finish doing all these steps, I am ready to begin my day.

▨ **Intermediate Exercise: Achieving Continuity**

Complete the paragraph below, beginning with the sentence already written. Write at least five more sentences and end with the one already written. Try to make every sentence in the passage follow from the one before.

> There are several ways to make friends in a new place. . . . If you try all of these techniques, you are sure to meet all the new friends you want.

■ **Challenge Exercise: Achieving Continuity**

Complete the paragraph below, beginning with the sentence already written. Write at least five more sentences and end with the one already written. Try to make every sentence in the passage follow from the one before.

> My favorite television show has several features that make it interesting. . . . All of these features together make it one of the best shows on television.

Proofreading Practice: Subordination

To achieve more variety in your sentence patterns, you should practice **subordination**. Subordination means using **subordinate clauses** to place some statements at a lower level of importance by beginning them with **subordinate conjunctions**. These are words that make the statement tell *how, when, where,* or *why* something happened, rather than *that* it happened. For example:

Main Clause (whole sentence: tells *that* something happened):

We arrived late. <u>An accident occurred on Route 87.</u>

Subordinate Clause (part of a sentence: tells *why* something happened):

We arrived late <u>because an accident occurred on Route 87.</u>

<u>Because an accident occurred on Route 87,</u> we arrived late.

When you begin a statement with *after, although, as, because, even though, since, when, whenever, whereas, wherever,* or *while,* you are making it a subordinate clause. Such clauses can begin sentences or end them, as in the example above. If your sentences seem too mechanical and repetitious, you may be able to improve your style by using more subordination.

TEST YOURSELF: SUBORDINATION

Underline the subordinate clauses in these sentences. One sentence has no subordinate clause.

1. Whenever Jennifer drives past the mall, she wants to stop and look at the sales.

2. James knew he would pass the course because he had reviewed for the final exam.

3. As winter approached, the fuel prices began to rise.

4. The film began while Jason was buying popcorn.

5. Although most people like Amy, few of her friends understand her.

6. The management decided against using a wireless network, whereas their competitors were already doing so.

7. Jeremy began exercising a month ago and has now lost twelve pounds.

Answers: 1. Whenever Jennifer drives past the mall 2. because he had reviewed for the exam 3. As winter approached 4. while Jason was buying popcorn 5. Although most people like Amy 6. whereas their competitors were already doing so 7. no subordinate clause

Proofreading Exercises: Basic, Intermediate, Challenge

☐ Basic Exercise: Subordination

Read this passage and in the blanks write subordinate conjunctions such as *after, although, as, because, even though, since, when, whenever, whereas, wherever,* and *while.* Be sure that the ones you insert make sense and read smoothly.

Waverly is a rescuer of animals. She likes to collect injured and lost animals and makes some of them her pets. _____ she finds a bird with a damaged wing, she takes it in. _____ she is able to make it better, she lets it go. _____ she is constantly bringing in stray cats and dogs that are limping or injured, she often has as many as a dozen animals in her house. Most of them she has been able to place in other people's homes once they are well again. _____ some of her neighbors disapprove of her having so many pets, she doesn't care what other people think. _____ she began this project, she has, according to her count, saved more than a hundred small animals. She has had to look up a lot of information about small animals _____ she is in the process of feeding and caring for them. It is no surprise that her mother once suggested that she should become a veterinarian _____ she already knows so much about healing small creatures.

☐ Intermediate Exercise: Subordination

Rewrite this passage, converting the underlined statements to subordinate clauses and combining them with sentences before or after them. Use words such as *although, because, when, while,* etc. to change these statements to subordinate clauses.

<u>Karen is the president of her class.</u> She has to organize many activities and get other students to work on projects and committees.

<u>Some of the student leaders she works with are helpful and hard</u> <u>working.</u> Others are not. She has discovered that the best way to get others to be positive and contributing is to praise them for whatever they do well. <u>Samantha manages a Web site for the</u> <u>school.</u> Karen tells her how impressive it is. <u>Mike designs a poster</u> <u>for homecoming week.</u> She tells him how great it looks. Such remarks do not prevent her from offering constructive criticism. <u>It's needed.</u> <u>Karen has created a positive feeling in student gov-</u> <u>ernment.</u> She has been able to accomplish a lot. <u>Karen graduates</u> <u>from college in June.</u> Her leadership in student government will help her succeed in her new job.

■ Challenge Exercise: Subordination

Rewrite each of these passages, combining the short sentences by using subordination.

1. Some of the terms used by philosophers are simple and clear. Others are hard to define and used differently by different writers.

2. *Empiricism,* for instance, is not a controversial term. Its meaning is reasonably clear and simple. Applying it to particular philosophers may not be simple.

3. We call an analytical approach *empirical.* We generally refer to analysis based on evidence gained through experience.

4. On the other hand, a term like *existentialism* is harder to define. It has been used by thinkers in many different ways.

5. Terms used in theology are especially controversial. Their meanings are often connected to strong beliefs and feelings.

6. Recently coined words, such as *semiotics* and *deconstruction,* are even harder to define and understand. They continue to be useful and necessary in discussions of literature and the media.

7. Philosophers want the public to appreciate and understand their work. They should explain the meaning of their terminology simply and clearly.

CHAPTER 5

PUTTING ON THE FINAL TOUCHES

Improving Word Choice; Eliminating Wordiness

Be precise. Be concise. Precision means saying exactly what you mean. Conciseness means saying it as briefly as possible.

Before submitting your final draft, examine it sentence by sentence to see whether you can improve your choice of words. In the process of composing, it is wise not to stop to consider all the synonyms available to you, because doing so can distract you from your larger purpose. As a result, however, some of the words you chose probably weren't the best. As you carefully read your last draft, hunt for words that do not fit, either because their meaning, called the denotation, is a little off or because they create the wrong tone or suggestion, called the connotation. Some words have negative connotations, some positive, and some neutral. Be ready to substitute more accurate or suitable words for the ones you have written. Use your thesaurus, either in book form, such as an edition of *Roget's Thesaurus*, or as a word-processing function on your toolbar (click Tools, then Language, then Thesaurus).

Another way to improve your word choice is by reducing wordiness, which simply means removing unnecessary words. Wordiness doesn't mean writing a lot; it means using too many empty words, roundabout phrases, and pointless repetitions. Wordiness usually comes from an attempt to sound impressive rather than to communicate something important. When you have an urgent message, you are less likely to waste words conveying it. Wordiness can also come from not having enough to say but being required to write 500 or 1000 words for an assignment. When that happens, of course it is tempting to "pad" your essay with unnecessary words.

We've all read pieces that skirt around a topic and use pompous words and phrases but say very little that's new or thought-provoking. If you find yourself lapsing into that pattern, do not settle for merely tightening up your style. Rethink your main purpose; find some fresh ideas and examples. No display of fancy language can hide a lack of content.

Lack of conciseness often occurs in long sentences, particularly ones that express complicated ideas. Here is an example:

> In the story "The Lottery" by Shirley Jackson the author tells us about a woman who is the one chosen by lottery to be stoned and she protests that it is unfair to stone her but it is not because she objects to the outrageousness of the lottery which she does not but just because it was unfair that she was chosen instead of somebody else.

The problem with that sentence is not just that it is too long but that it is loose and baggy. Shorter, more concise sentences would be better:

> In "The Lottery" Shirley Jackson portrays a woman who is chosen by lottery to be stoned and who objects, not because the lottery is cruel, but because she is the victim.

TEST YOURSELF: ELIMINATING WORDINESS

Rewrite these sentences, making them more concise:

1. There are three ways by means of which you can travel to Chicago: you can ride there on the train, you can fly in an airplane, or you can drive in your own car on the highway.

2. In his poem entitled "The Raven," the author, Edgar Allan Poe, writes about a bird called a raven that keeps saying continually again and again the word "nevermore."

3. According to how much the test counts when the instructor figures out the final grades in the class, more psychological pressure the test puts on students when they take it.

4. Two people may think they love each other but do not really understand each other's true personalities and therefore are not really in love.

5. One point of similarity between the main characters in these two stories is that they are both women who have vivid imaginations and they are both unhappy women as well.

6. We will never find a solution to this problem unless and until the parties on both sides find it in their hearts to go half way and begin to see it from the other person's point of view and reach a compromise.

7. The length of the readings in this assignment adds up to a lot more than most people would be able to finish reading over a single weekend.

Possible answers: 1. You can travel to Chicago by train, airplane, or car. 2. In Edgar Allan Poe's poem "The Raven," a bird repeats the word "nevermore." 3. The more the test counts as a percentage of the final grade, the greater the stress it places on students. 4. True love is possible only between people who understand each other. 5. In both stories the main characters are imaginative but unhappy women. 6. This problem can be solved only if both parties are willing to compromise. 7. This reading assignment is too long to complete in one weekend.

Proofreading Aloud; Locating Your Patterns of Error

Proofreading requires patience and close attention. It is a kind of courtesy you pay to your readers. Many people do not proofread their e-mail messages, which is O.K. when you are informally e-mailing friends. Formal academic essays require more care, however. To proofread effectively, read your work aloud, s-l-o-w-l-y. This isn't the time to rush; if you do, you may miss errors that you could easily correct. In addition, reading aloud will help you identify sentence divisions. When your voice drops, that is probably the end of a sentence: Be sure to place a period there. Reading aloud also helps you feel the rhythm, or lack of rhythm, in your writing. If something in your writing bothers you when you read aloud, try reading it to someone else; perhaps that person can help you identify the problem.

One purpose of reading aloud is to help you notice recurring patterns in your writing. Do you frequently run sentences together or write fragments? Do you make errors in verb form that you can hear, such as "you was" or "she has went"? Many of our writing errors are not random, but fit into a few patterns that occur frequently.

Using Your Spelling and Grammar Check

Technology is helpful when it comes to correcting writing errors, but you must not rely on it alone to catch and correct mistakes, because it can create as well as correct problems. Using your spelling and grammar checks is a must. The spelling check will catch most typos and misspellings, but it cannot identify word-choice errors. For instance, it cannot catch *their* instead of *there*. There is another danger in relying totally on your word processor's spelling check: that you will not become a good speller.

Grammar checks are still not reliable. They identify some errors but not others, and they often see errors that do not exist. Do not substitute the grammar check for your own sound grasp of grammar. Instead, use the grammar check only as backup after you have done your own careful proofreading.

WRITING TIP #5

Making final touches on an essay takes care and pride in your work. Instead of thinking of your essay as a sculpture that is carved in stone and cannot be altered, realize that the difference is in the details: any essay can be improved by making an additional chip here or smoothing a rough edge there. If you are satisfied with the overall organization and content of your work, assume that you can find word choices to improve and sentences to tighten up. Remove deadwood. Sharpen vague statements. You are already a competent writer, but polish your essay to make it the very best it can be.

Writing Exercises: Basic, Intermediate, Chal

☐ **Basic Exercise: Putting on the Final Touches**

Read the passage below and revise the underlined words or phrases, either eliminating wordiness or making corrections in spelling or grammar.

<u>In my opinion, I feel</u> that most of my classmates would like <u>there</u> campus to be more user-friendly. Most of the students realizes that <u>often it is usually</u> difficult to go from one class to another and get there <u>on time without being late.</u> The student government has <u>propose</u> a new schedule that would leave 15 minutes between classes. That way students would not feel to pressured and would not have to hurry all the time.

■ **Intermediate Exercise: Putting on the Final Touches**

Read the passage below and revise the underlined words or phrases, either eliminating wordiness or making corrections in spelling or grammar.

Many people have strong <u>emotional feelings</u> about using stem cells for medical research. <u>It is a fact that</u> some people argue that progress toward finding cures for Parkinson's disease and other serious <u>illness</u> can go forward only if embryonic stem cells are <u>use.</u> Other people raise religious objections and <u>insists</u> that using embryos violates the <u>holy sanctity</u> of human life. Candidates for public office sometimes try to use this controversy to gain votes, and talk show debates often flare up on the subject. People on <u>both sides of the issue, pro and con,</u> should know more about the scientific facts involved.

■ **Challenge Exercise: Putting on the Final Touches**

Rewrite the passage below, eliminating wordiness and making corrections in spelling or grammar.

In "The Guest," a short story written by the author Albert Camus, a schoolteacher named Daru is ordered to guard an Arab prisoner. This man has killed someone, and Daru is suppose to take him to prison. Daru does not want to become involved, and he treats the Arab man as a guest rather than a prisoner. Instead of taking him to jail, Daru take the prisoner outside and points in two directions, one leading to prison and the other to freedom. The Arab walks off toward the prison alone by himself. When Daru returns back to his schoolroom, he reads an angry message written on the board. Even though he did not turn the prisoner in, the prisoner friends threaten to take revenge. This story expresses the author's disgust at violence and also in addition his belief in the freedom of the individual to make choices in an absurd world.

Proofreading Practice: Spelling

To become a better speller, take charge of the problem yourself. Many writing courses do not devote much time to spelling, so you cannot expect classwork alone to improve your spelling ability. Do not expect to improve without making repeated effort. Only a few people can spell correctly without effort; the rest of us need to do old-fashioned work on the words we often misspell.

How can you improve your spelling?

- Learn the patterns and rules. Although English spelling is irregular, and most of its rules have exceptions, you will do well to recognize some basic patterns.

- Drill on frequently misspelled words. Study tricky words, or spelling "demons," especially those in your area of work or study. A corporate employee should never misspell *business* or a nurse misspell *medicine*.

- Use your spell check effectively but do not trust it totally. The better a speller you are, the more your spell check will help you catch typos. However, it will miss many words called homonyms: words that sound alike and look alike but have different meanings. Therefore,

- Master the look-alikes/sound-alikes. A large percentage of misspellings come from words being confused with others that look or sound almost like them.

- Take personal responsibility for your spelling. Do not expect a book, a course, a teacher, or spell check to work magic for you. It is up to you; make lists of your own most often misspelled words and study them.

Spelling Patterns

The first step toward spelling competence is to learn the main patterns of English, even though they may have exceptions.

Pattern 1: ie and ei Words You probably have heard, and may know, the old rule:

> i before e
> except after c
> or when sounded like a
> as in neighbor or weigh.

Knowing the jingle helps, but be prepared for the many exceptions. Study the patterns.

1. i before e: Believe. Most words with an e sound do follow the rule when there is no c before the combination:

   achieve (ch, but not c)   pierce

   friend (even though pronounced eh)   priest

   fiend   relieve

   grieve   reprieve

   lien   retrieve

   niece (the c comes after ie)   shriek

   piece   thief

2. Except after c: Receive. Despite exceptions, this pattern usually holds true, too:

   ceiling, conceited, conceive, deceive, perceive, receipt

3. Or when sounded like a: Weigh. Combinations that are sounded like a or i are usually ei:

   eight, freight, height, neighbor, vein, weight

   Some exceptions to the rule: A few words take ie even though it comes after c:

   financier, society, species

4. A few ei words with the e sound and no c before them can fool you, too:

> either, leisure, neither, seize, weird

Pattern 2: Keeping or Dropping the Final e When adding an ending to a word with a final e, keep the e if the ending starts with a consonant:

> arrange + ment = arrangement
>
> hope + ful = hopeful
>
> nine + ty = ninety
>
> sincere + ly = sincerely
>
> face + less = faceless
>
> manage + ment = management

Drop the e if the ending starts with a vowel:

> give + ing = giving
>
> have + ing = having
>
> erase + ure = erasure
>
> locate + ion = location
>
> guide + ance = guidance

Exceptions: To keep a g or c soft before a vowel, we sometimes keep the e:

> age + ing = ageing or aging
>
> manage + able = manageable
>
> service + able = serviceable

The word *judgment* does not keep the e except in British spelling. *Dyeing* keeps the e to prevent confusion with *dying*.

Pattern 3: Doubling Final Consonants This rule is somewhat complicated, but it does not have many exceptions and it includes many common words. Learn the pattern.

The rule applies to words like begin, control, and occur. When you add an *ed*, *ing*, or *er* ending to these words, do you double the final consonant? Yes: *beginning*, *controlled*, and *occurred*.

What do these words have in common? The rule says that they end with a single consonant (not ck as in shock, or st as in post) preceded by a single vowel (not a double vowel, as in break or meet). And the accent must be on the last syllable (not earlier, as in travel, where the l does not have to be doubled, or pivot, where the t is not doubled).

To sum up, these words contain

- A single final consonant: be<u>gin</u>
- A single vowel preceding the final consonant: beg<u>i</u>n
- An accent on the last syllable: be<u>gin</u>

Many common words follow this pattern. When you become familiar with it, the rule is extremely useful. Here are only some of the examples:

beginning	forgetting	referred
committed	occurring	stopped*
controlling	omitted	throbbing*
excelling	preferring	

*The rule applies to one-syllable words as well.

TEST YOURSELF: SPELLING PATTERNS

Some of the following words are correct, and some are misspelled. Write C next to the correct ones, and spell the others correctly in the blanks. Review the rules first; try not to guess.

1. belief _____   5. commited _____

2. occurance _____   6. movement _____

3. arrangment _____   7. achieve _____

4. definitly _____

Answers: 1. correct 2. occurrence 3. arrangement 4. definitely 5. committed 6. correct 7. correct

Twenty Common Mix-ups

The following words are often misspelled because they contain combinations that are easily confused with those in similar words. Study the groups carefully, looking for the trouble spots.

1. ability   (The last two do not contain *ability*.)
   responsibility
   possibility

2. accumulate   (Study the c's and m's in these common
   accommodate   words.)
   recommend

3. across   (Both are often misspelled; notice the single
   address   c and double d.)

4. alone   (Two simple words but often carelessly
   along   mixed up.)

5. amount   (Be careful not to write *amoung*, even
   among   though among rhymes with *young*.)

6. arithmetic   (Not *atheletics* or *athelete*, and don't forget
   athletics   the e in *mathematics*.)
   mathematics

7. believe   (These two most common ie/ei words do
   receive   follow the rule.)

8. committee   (Note the single t in *commitment*.)
   committing
   commitment

9. definitely   (Do not confuse –itely with –ately words.)
   immediately

10. develop   (There is no such word as *develope*.)
    developed
    envelope

11. divide   (Not *devide*)
    decide

12. familiar   (The extra i in familiar gives it an extra
    similar   syllable.)

13. fulfill   (Do not spell it *forfill* or *forefill*.)
    foretell

14. necessary   (Only one c in *necessary*, one s in *occasion-*
    occasionally   *ally*, and one f in *professional*.)
    professional

15. pastime   (Do not double that t in *pastime*.)
    part-time

16. accidentally   (Not *publically*)
      publicly

17. relevant   (Two difficult words; notice the e's and a's
      prevalent   and the l's and v's. Both words contain the
      name Eva.)

18. separate   (Not *seperate*)
      desperate

19. surprise   (Do not write *suprise* or *surpose*.)
      suppose

20. till   (Not *untill*)
      until

TEST YOURSELF: SPELLING MIX-UPS

Each of the following groups contains one misspelled word. Circle
it and write the word correctly in the blank.

1. adress
   necessary   _____
   till

2. accomodate
   publicly   _____
   fulfill

3. prevalent
   receive   _____
   surpose

4. desperate
   pastime   _____
   devide

5. occassionally
   familiar   _____
   across

6. responsability
   professional   _____
   recommend

7. definitely
   possibility   _____
   amoung

Answers: 1. address 2. accommodate 3. suppose 4. divide 5. occasionally 6. responsibility 7. among

Proofreading Exercises: Basic, Intermediate, Challenge

☐ Basic Exercise: Spelling

The paragraph below contains seven misspelled common words. Find and correct them.

> Paula and Beverly wanted to arrange a baby shower for there friend Annette. They had similiar ideas about how to plan the event, but they couldn't decide on were it should take place. Each of them beleived it should be held at her home as a supprise party. Finally, since they couldn't dicide, they tossed a coin, and Beverly won. Then they got together and made the necessary arrangments.

▣ Intermediate Exercise: Spelling

The following paragraph contains seven misspelled words. Find and correct them.

> Writing well is a skill that you should develope to help you in your career. In business, law, and medicine, effective writing is neccessary. Students who do not beleive this is true are often surprised to discover too late that they lack this important proffesional competency. They may have to learn the hard way—by recieving criticism of their work—that writing well is expected on many jobs. In the business world it is understood that the committment to writing goes along with the strickly technical aspects of a job.

■ Challenge Exercise: Spelling

The paragraph below contains seven misspelled common words. Find and correct them.

> Many scholars have puzzled over the extraordinary developement of Shakespeare as a poet and playwright. There was little in his imediate surroundings as a boy and an adolescent that could explain his astonishing achievments as possibly the world's great-

est writer. He was probably educated strickly and traditionally at the school in his hometown of Stratford, but his experience in theater was probably limited to performing plays at school and watching traveling companies of actors that occassionally visited his hometown. We will probably never know what brought him to London and lead him to join the theater companies there. We do know that he became highly sucessful as a writer and part owner of the theater. When he retired to Stratford, he bought the largest house in town.

STEP TWO

WRITING ESSAYS BASED ON YOUR OWN EXPERIENCE AND PERCEPTIONS

CHAPTER 6
DESCRIBING A SITUATION, PERSON, OR GROUP

Visualizing Your Subject and Giving It Meaning

Descriptive writing is like drawing and painting with words. But words are not pictures; your readers have to imagine everything you describe. Unlike pictures, words require readers to use all five senses in their imaginations. To describe a person, place, or group well, use specific, concrete language to create in readers' minds the most vivid experience you can.

Like drawing and painting, descriptive writing has meaning. A picture or an essay conveys a message through what it portrays. A portrait or photograph may make you feel sad, excited, puzzled, or angry; a descriptive essay may cause you to admire, like, or detest a person. Whether or not you announce your meaning, the way you describe something will have meaning and will affect your readers. In order to create the impression you want, read an early draft aloud to several friends or writing group members to discover whether you are creating the impression you intend.

Student Essay: Describing a Person

My Abuelita
Lourdes Fernández

The person who has influenced me the most has been my grandma, my Abuelita. She has done a lot of good things for me in my life, and she taught me a lot, but some of her ways were hard for me to accept. She was always there for me, sometimes when nobody else was, and I will always be thankful for her help in my life. She was my angel, although sometimes I used to think she was my bad angel. I now realize that she was always strong, loyal, and wise.

First let me tell you the good things about my Abuelita. She is a very big person, but not in height, only in the person she is. She can be described as strong emotionally and spiritually. She came to the United States from the Dominican Republic without speaking any English. She worked in Washington, D.C., cleaning people's houses until she met my grandfather. He got a job in New York City, so they moved there and had six children. She had the strength to raise all of them to be educated and hard workers, and all the time she worked long hours. Sometimes she did sewing at home, and later she cooked in a restaurant, and on weekends she was on the cleaning staff in an office building. No matter how hard things got, she never gave up, and she always found ways to solve problems.

I call her loyal because when her children got in trouble or didn't do well in school, she always supported them. When they were wrong, she didn't let them get away with it, but she always let them know she loved them and would do anything to help them get their problem solved. And with me she became my number one parent when my dad was out of the country and my mom was in and out of the hospital. She gave me many words of wisdom, telling me that all I had to do was imagine where I wanted to be in life and hold onto that dream until I finally made it come true. She told me stories about people in Santo Domingo and corrected my Spanish. She made me feel smart and successful even when I had trouble with my chemistry class and when I ran for student vice president and lost. Nobody was ever more helpful to me.

Maybe this sounds like she was perfect and we always got along. That isn't true. She still has some ways that I don't agree with. She was very old-fashioned in her thinking and usually disapproved of my choices and opinions. She wouldn't let me date until I was sixteen, and she frowned at most of the clothes I wanted to wear. She said they made me look like a loose woman and she sometimes would forbid me to leave the house until I changed into something "proper for a lady." And she hated almost all the music I liked and tried to teach me all the religious songs she sang every day. My first boyfriend she wouldn't let into the house because she called him a good-for-nothing and a bum. After I stopped seeing him I partly agreed with her, but still I didn't like the way she criticized me about him.

I now know that she was only trying to do what was best for me and teach me right from wrong. Even when we disagreed, she always loved me and wanted me to reach my goals. She will always be in my heart as the person who helped me become the person I am. When I have children, I want to be a parent just like her, except maybe I'll have better taste in clothes and music.

Lourdes found a way to organize the body of her essay into two main parts, which she divided into separate paragraphs. First she described the good things about her grandmother in two paragraphs; then she described the traits that were not so good in another paragraph. There are a number of ways you can organize a descriptive essay. Which of the patterns mentioned below did Lourdes use?

Organizing a Description

Descriptive essays can be organized in different ways. They can be arranged **spatially**, meaning that you move from front to back, side to side, far to near, and so on. Or, you can use a **chronological arrangement**, or arrangement in time, showing how a person has changed from childhood to maturity, or how you experienced the situation or place you want to describe, beginning with your first impressions and moving to a time when you understood it more clearly. Still another possibility is to arrange your material **topically**, according to different features of the subject, such as a person's appearance, personality, and accomplishments. Early drafts of a descriptive essay are often jumbled, as you try to include all the important details about your subject. This initial chaos is fine, but be sure that your later drafts have a clear plan of organization. In descriptive writing, revision usually entails a lot of rearranging.

Here is a description of a place. What plan or organization does it follow, and what details make the description memorable?

Example by a Published Author: Using Details

How beautiful, she thought. What a beautiful house. There was a big red-and-gold Bible on the dining-room table. Little lace doilies were everywhere—on arms and backs of chairs, in the center of a large dining table, on little tables. Potted plants were on all the windowsills. A color picture of Jesus Christ hung on a wall with the prettiest paper flowers fastened on the frame. She wanted to see everything slowly, slowly. But Junior kept saying, "Hey you. Come on. Come on." He pulled her into another room, even more beautiful than the first. More doilies, a big lamp with green-and-gold base and white shade. There was even a rug on the floor, with enormous dark-red flowers. She was deep in admiration of the flowers when Junior said, "Here!" Pecola turned. "Here is your kitten!" he screeched. And he threw a big black cat right in her face. She sucked in her breath in fear and surprise and felt fur in her mouth. The cat clawed her face and chest in an effort to right itself, then leaped nimbly to the floor. (89–90)

—Toni Morrison. From *The Bluest Eye*.

What do the details of the interior of the house tell you about the people who live there? What does that description make you feel? Pecola, a young girl in the novel, experiences two opposing feelings in this paragraph. Explain what these feelings are and identify details that communicate each emotion.

> ## WRITING TIP #6
> You have probably been told to "include a lot of details" in your writing, especially descriptive writing. That can be good or bad advice, depending on the details you choose to include. Writing is not photography; you cannot capture every detail in your subject, so you have to carefully select which ones to include. Descriptive writing is more like drawing a cartoon or sketch that captures and highlights the most recognizable and characteristic features of your subject. The point is to create a distinct impression of the person, place, or organization you describe. You will succeed best if you remember to include details—the important ones, not all of them.

Writing Exercises: Basic, Intermediate, Challenge

☐ Basic Exercise: Descriptive Writing

Write an essay describing a place that you visit frequently. This may be an office where you work, a gymnasium where you work out, a store or mall where you shop, or a diner where you eat. Think first of the feeling this place arouses in you. Then, using a prewriting activity that works for you, select the details that most strongly evoke this feeling. After writing a first draft, find a way to organize your material, either by moving from one location to another (near to far, right to left, etc.) or by clustering your details according to the senses (sounds, visual impressions, smells, etc.) or according to other categories (obvious details, less noticeable details, and details that create false impressions). Use your creative powers in selecting categories and in choosing descriptive vocabulary.

▦ Intermediate Exercise: Descriptive Writing

Write an essay portraying a person who has had a powerful influence on your life. Begin with a focused writing exercise in which you write freely for several pages about this person, jotting down everything that comes to mind about him or her. Look over your work and identify what it is about that person that has influenced you for good or bad, or both. Organize your material by clustering, cubing, or outlining, so that you can bring out different aspects of this person's character and behavior. Quote or paraphrase (put in your own words) this person's most memorable sayings, and describe how this person behaves in different situations. If the person's physical qualities affected his or her influence on you, be sure to describe them as well. Remember to make your introduction and conclusion especially vivid as you create a complete impression of this person in the reader's mind.

▰ Challenge Exercise: Descriptive Writing

Describe a course you have taken and completed, either in high school or in college. First collect all the facts about this course you can think of, either by brainstorming or by doing several pages of focused writing. Then identify your main point about this course—what you gained from it and why it is worth describing. Group your material using a cluster or cubing exercise, sorting out different aspects of the course, such as the teacher's style, your relation to your classmates, the books and other materials used, the course content, the skills required, and the facts and insights you acquired. In your revised draft, be sure that your introduction and conclusion state clearly and emphatically what made your experience of taking this course worth writing about.

Essay Topics: Descriptive Writing

1. Describe a natural scene that inspires you
2. Describe a person who deserves to be better known
3. Describe an organization or team of which you have been a member
4. Describe a character on your favorite television program
5. Describe a painting, statue, or special exhibit in a museum near you
6. Describe a storm that you witnessed
7. Describe a recent invention that has made life better

PEER REVIEW QUESTIONS: DESCRIPTIVE WRITING

1. Here is the impression I think you are trying to convey in your description:
2. Your introduction is interesting.   ☐ yes   ☐ no
   Your introduction makes your attitude toward your topic clear.   ☐ yes   ☐ no
   The sentence that most nearly expresses this attitude is the following:
3. You create an overall impression well.   ☐ yes   ☐ no
4. The following details create a vivid impression of your subject:
5. Your conclusion (is/is not) effective for the following reason:
6. What I like best about your description is the following:
7. I recommend you make the following changes:

Proofreading Practice: Adjectives and Adverbs

People often confuse adjectives with adverbs, and vice versa.

Telling the Difference Between Adjectives and Adverbs

The most common mistake people make with adjectives and adverbs is to write *good* when they mean *well*.

Not: This engine runs good.

But: This engine runs well.

Good is an adjective; *well* is an adverb. What is the difference?

Adjectives tell *which, what kind of,* or *how many*; they modify nouns or pronouns:

a perfect evening   a foolish idea

the final chapter   a rapid message

Adverbs tell *how, when,* and *where*; they modify verbs, adjectives, and other adverbs:

The evening went perfectly.   He acted foolishly.

They finally arrived.   She talked rapidly.

Another common mistake is to omit the *ly* ending on adverbs. Many adjectives can be converted into adverbs by adding *ly*.

Adjective	Adverb
a quick meal	We ate the meal quickly.
a real diamond	a really fine diamond
a bad feeling	They arranged it badly.
The answer was correct.	They answered correctly.

Remember to use **adjectives** after forms of *be* (*is, are, was, were*). Adjectives in this case modify the subject. Also use **adjectives** after verbs of the senses such as *feel, smell, sound,* and *taste.*

1. The film sounds exciting. (*Exciting* modifies *film.*)
2. The pastry smells delicious. (*Delicious* modifies *pastry.*)

3. I feel <u>good</u> this morning. (*Good* modifies *I*.)

4. The bread tastes <u>stale</u>. (*Stale* modifies *bread*.)

Do not confuse these adjectives (called **predicate adjectives** because they come after the verb, not before the noun) with **adverbs** that come after verbs.

1. The script reads <u>smoothly</u>. (*Smoothly* modifies *reads*.)

2. The chef makes pastry <u>expertly</u>. (*Expertly* modifies *makes*.)

3. I dress <u>quickly</u> in the morning. (*Quickly* modifies *dress*.)

4. She writes stories <u>frequently</u>. (*Frequently* modifies *writes*.)

Some Tricky Adverbs Certain adverbs are often confused with adjectives. Be on the lookout for these:

Adjective	Adverb
<u>most</u> people	<u>almost</u> always
She feels <u>bad</u>.	She sings <u>badly</u>.
an <u>easy</u> job	He does it <u>easily</u>.
an <u>everyday</u> task	He swims <u>every day</u>.
a <u>slow</u> pace	Drive <u>slowly</u>. (*Slow* also accepted as an adverb.)

TEST YOURSELF: ADJECTIVES AND ADVERBS

Choose the correct form in each sentence.

1. Day care workers have to be (real, really) mature.

2. These computer games help children learn (easy, easily).

3. Some people feel (bad, badly) after their favorite teams lose.

4. Pilates exercises have become an (everyday, every day) activity for many people.

5. Toner cartridges are (most, almost, mostly) as expensive as printers themselves.

6. Some children behave (violent, violently) after their parents argue.

7. To choose a major (careful, carefully), you should talk to students in the program.

Answers: 1. really 2. easily 3. bad 4. everyday 5. almost 6. violently 7. carefully

Proofreading Exercises: Basic, Intermediate, Challenge

☑ Basic Exercise: Adjectives and Adverbs

Practice using *good* and *well* correctly: write the adjective *good* or the adverb *well* in each blank. Remember that *well* may be an adjective meaning "healthy," or "not sick."

1. Jessica did the assignment _____.

2. She had a _____ memory and could write _____.

3. After being absent during an illness, she had gotten _____ again; now she was expecting to earn a _____ grade on the final exam.

4. It felt _____ to have a challenging task.

5. She remembered _____ how hard high school had been.

6. A career in some medical field now looked _____ to her.

7. It was a _____ way to help people and it paid _____.

▣ Intermediate Exercise: Adjectives and Adverbs

Supply the missing forms.

Adjective	Adverb
Example: She is <u>stylish</u>.	She dresses <u>stylishly</u>.
1. His reply was <u>slow</u>.	He replied _____.
2. The problem was <u>easy</u>.	She solved the problem _____.
3. The ending was _____.	The play ended <u>happily</u>.
4. We gave it <u>careful</u> thought.	We considered it _____.

5. He felt _____ about   He did the job <u>badly</u>.
   the job.

6. They created a <u>good</u> plan.   They planned _____.

7. The supervisor was <u>efficient</u>.   She supervised the office
   _____.

■ Challenge Exercise: Adjectives and Adverbs

Compose sentences using the following words and phrases.

1. good   4. probable   7. everyday
   well   probably   every day   *odd*

2. especially   5. careful
   special   carefully

3. bad   6. real
   badly   really

CHAPTER 7

TELLING A STORY TO MAKE A POINT

Organizing Chronologically

Telling a story, or **narration**, is one of the most important ways of developing an idea. It can be the easiest way to organize material, because narration is simply telling about a series of events in the order in which they occurred. Often, however, your story will not be that simple. Probably, parts of it need to be told in detail, minute by minute, while other parts can be skipped. One paragraph may concentrate on an important moment, while another may sum up events that happen over several months or years. Sometimes you want to include quoted conversations or to pause and describe a person or situation. Narrative rarely moves like clockwork, at a steady, measured pace; in fact it may even begin near the end of the events, flash back, tell a story, then work its way to where the story concludes. Although narrative writing can be one of the simpler modes, it also can be quite complex. Be ready to rethink and revise your story to emphasize its effect on your reader and the meaning you want the reader to derive from it.

Telling a Meaningful and Moving Story

Many people write memoirs, and it is sometimes said that every human being's life contains a novel. That is, everyone's life has meaning, and if the story were told well, readers would grasp that meaning and respond emotionally to it. The way you tell a story is what gives it meaning. The best novels and short stories are read and reread because they are especially rich in meaning. Make the story you tell so full of meaning and emotional impact that the reader will want to read it again. Your first draft may flow easily as you simply tell your story. But then you should read it a day or two later as if someone else wrote it. Which parts need to be dramatized more? Which section moves too slowly? How can you experiment with the time sequence to create suspense, distance, uncertainty, or emphasis?

Student Essay: Telling a Story to Make a Point

This essay was written by a student who uses a story of his experience in the military to examine his own attitudes. Rodney Vega uses narrative development to support an important point about himself and about tolerance in relating to others. In doing that, he makes his essay meaningful to anyone reading it, since we have all had to reflect on things in ourselves that may need improvement. This essay does not show all the stages of the writing process that Rodney went through. As a successful final draft, it provides the kind of goal to aim for. The essay tells a story but also, like all effective essays, makes an important point. Notice that the essay has a clear introduction, thesis, and conclusion, and several paragraphs begin with topic sentences that guide the reader.

A Weighty Experience
Rodney Vega

Introduction

Throughout my military career, I traveled to many places and had encounters with all sorts of people. Some were religious, others atheist; some were tough, others timid; some were bright, others not quite. However, I was never prejudiced toward anyone regardless of these varied characteristics. When it came to physical appearance, however—in terms of one's weight—it was a completely different issue. I despised overweight people and considered them both lazy and careless, particularly if they were in the military. In addition, to me, being overweight was a liability. I would have hated to lose someone in combat simply because they couldn't keep their grubby little fingers out of the cookie jar. *So I thought, until I had an experience that totally changed my attitude toward overweight people.*

**Thesis
Statement**

Shortly after my promotion to sergeant, I was assigned to train a unit of fifteen recruits who were deemed "unfit" by Marine Corps regulations. I wasn't enthusiastic about the assignment, but it did present a golden opportunity: not only could I show off my outstanding physical conditioning, but I was also allowed to mock the overweight soldiers. I searched on the Internet for "fat" jokes and insults I could use the next day. Not surprisingly, a group of trainees soon complained to the department officer about my training techniques, claiming that they could not stand my verbal abuse anymore.

**Body
Paragraphs
Using Narrative
to Support a
Thesis**

The officer immediately called me in to discuss my methods. I argued that my training techniques were within regulations and involved the same psychological methods that drill instructors use to motivate overweight recruits. He did not dispute my argument and allowed me to continue with my training methods. After several months, new soldiers were assigned to my squad while others passed the program and were processed out. However, I had become intensely disliked by many and even overheard rumors of people making obscene puns on my name. But I didn't care; in fact, I pushed even harder.

Topic Sentence

My sense of superiority, however, was soon to be challenged. One morning a new soldier appeared unexpectedly in my unit. Anxious as always to show off in front of new people, I was more intense in training than ever. I enjoyed scaring the "Twinkies," as I called the newly assigned overweight soldiers. We began that morning as usual jogging at a slow pace for two miles while I shouted cadences about cakes, Krispy Kreme doughnuts, and ice cream. Then I made everyone do the standard Marine Corps three-mile run to test their individual fitness. My true intention, of course, was to humiliate the new individual. As always, I was far ahead of everyone on the track, but after the first mile, something happened. To my amazement, someone was closing in on me, and fast. I couldn't believe it: it was the newbie! There was no way I was going to be beaten, so I gave it my all. But after two miles the new recruit was sitting at the finish line waiting for me.

Topic Sentence   *In the attempt to redeem my pride, I tried to deny what was happening.* I claimed that I had severe stomach pains. How could I admit that a "fat body" had defeated me in a race? And to make matters worse, the fat body was a young woman who had given birth just a few weeks before! I cancelled training for the next two days, claiming that I needed to recover from the stomach pains. At our next meeting, I tried even harder, running like a train down the track; but to my extreme disappointment, she arrived at the finish line before me again. After one more humiliating loss, knowing that everyone in my division was silently mocking me, I began to admire her persistence and determination—and I began to like her too.

Topic Sentence   *I tried a new way of making an impression.* I ceased the verbal hazing and began treating the recruits with respect as real Marines. Everyone was surprised and wondered what caused my change of heart. They soon began to think highly of me. That, however, was just a bonus, as my real intention was to win the friendship of the young woman. As the days and weeks passed, I formed friendships with some of the people in my program by treating them as people just like me. As I got to know them, I realized that some were struggling with depression or medical conditions. They were not all sitting in bed with cheesecake and Doritos watching television. After listening to their stories, I became sympathetic toward their situations.

Conclusion

After seven months, I was replaced by a new sergeant and went on to other assignments. *In the process of training others, I was the one who changed the most.* The people whom I once ridiculed and made stereotypes of had not only proven themselves capable of enduring my rigorous training but had convinced me that I was no more special than they were. Because they helped me see my true self and what I had become, they in a sense saved me from myself. I've learned to accept others because of that invaluable experience. However, even though I gained much from that experience, I never succeeded in obtaining what I set out to get by changing my attitudes and behavior: I never got to date the young woman.

1. In your own words, explain the main lesson of Rodney's essay.
2. What change takes place in his attitudes, and what causes the change?
3. Approximately how much time elapses in the period covered by the essay?
4. Identify details that Rodney includes to give the essay interest and humor.
5. How does he use the element of surprise to hold your interest?
6. How does his introduction pull you into the story?
7. What does his final paragraph add to the story?

Example by a Published Author

Here is a narrative that covers a long period of time in a few words and contains a lesson:

The Tunnel

Zenkai, the son of a samurai, journeyed to Edo and there became the retainer of a high official. He fell in love with the official's wife and was discovered. In self-defense, he slew the official. Then he ran away with the wife.

Both of them later became thieves. But the woman was so greedy that Zenkai grew disgusted. Finally, leaving her, he journeyed far away to the province of Buzen, where he became a wandering mendicant.

To atone for his past, Zenkai resolved to accomplish some good deed in his lifetime. Knowing of a dangerous road over a cliff that had caused the death and injury of many persons, he resolved to cut a tunnel through the mountain there.

Begging food in the daytime, Zenkai worked at night digging his tunnel. When thirty years had gone by, the tunnel was 2,280 feet long, 20 feet high, and 30 feet wide.

Two years before the work was completed, the son of the official he had slain, who was a skillful swordsman, found Zenkai out and came to kill him in revenge.

"I will give you my life willingly," said Zenkai. "Only let me finish this work. On the day it is completed, then you may kill me."

So the son awaited the day. Several months passed and Zenkai kept on digging. The son grew tired of doing nothing and began to help with the digging. After he had helped for more than a year, he came to admire Zenkai's strong will and character.

At last the tunnel was completed and the people could use it and travel in safety.

"Now cut off my head," said Zenkai. "My work is done."

"How can I cut off my own teacher's head?" asked the younger man with tears in his eyes.

—from *Zen Flesh, Zen Bones: A Collection of Zen and Pre-Zen Writings.* Compiled by Paul Reps.

---

1. How much time does this story encompass?
2. Explain why Zenkai and the younger man do what they do.
3. What changes take place in the attitudes of both men?
4. Explain how the writer uses paragraphs to cover different periods of time.
5. Explain why he uses quotations at the end of the story.

6. This story is called a **parable**. Such stories, usually very short, occur in the Bible and folk literature and convey a message through narrative. Try to sum up the point of this parable. Does it have more than one lesson?

7. The author of this parable is no longer identifiable. Does it change your view of a story if its author is anonymous?

WRITING TIP #7

When you tell a story, do not assume that your narrative has to march along with regular, clock-like regularity. You will want to use your "fast forward" button at times, your "pause" button at others, and occasionally even your "rewind" button. Try reading a story such as Faulkner's "A Rose for Emily" to see how a great writer moves skillfully back and forth in time.

Writing Exercises: Basic, Intermediate, Challenge

☐ Basic Exercise: Narrative Writing

Write an essay telling the story of a trip you have taken. Arrange the story in chronological sequence: before, during, and after, or getting there, being there, and returning. Although this is one of the simplest ways of organizing an essay, it requires some balancing of the parts: Do not spend all of your time telling the reader how you got to your destination, leaving no time for the rest of the story. On the other hand, do not neglect to tell the reader what you did when you were at the place you visited or what your return trip was like. Although this will be a story that includes many facts, it should have an overall point. First write a draft telling about the trip, then look it over and decide what you gained from the experience, and make this point in your introduction and conclusion.

■ Intermediate Exercise: Narrative Writing

Write an essay in which you relate an important change in your life. This may be a change of living circumstances, relationship (such as marriage or divorce), employment, physical appearance or health, or membership in a group (either joining or leaving). Develop each part of the story fully: explain the circumstances that led to the change, tell about how you felt during the change, and analyze what that change has meant in your life. You will probably need to write several drafts to ensure that each part is detailed enough and complete, so that the whole story is told. Your introduction and conclusion should help the reader identify with the meaning of the experience.

■ Challenge Exercise: Narrative Writing

Write your intellectual and philosophical autobiography. Tell how your opinions developed during an important part of your life, such as childhood or adolescence. Identify clearly what opinions you now hold on politics, religion, family, and careers. Explain what influences caused you to have your early opinions and what caused them to grow and change. Your introduction and conclusion should make your memoir interesting to the reader and meaningful to anyone.

Essay Topics: Narration

1. Tell the story of an important relationship in your life and how it changed.

2. Tell about an experience in which you met a challenge successfully.

3. Tell about a job experience from which you learned something.

4. Tell about buying a product or service that you were dissatisfied with.

5. Tell about an experience of being in the hospital.

6. Tell about the experience of finding a place to live.

7. Tell about the experience of meeting a famous person.

PEER REVIEW QUESTIONS: NARRATIVE WRITING

1. Here is the point I think you are making in your story:

2. Your introduction is interesting. ☐ yes ☐ no
   Your introduction and conclusion make your point clear.
   ☐ yes ☐ no
   The sentence that most nearly expresses your point is the following:

3. Your story is interesting and easy to follow. ☐ yes ☐ no

4. Each paragraph in your essay moves the story one step further toward a climax. ☐ yes ☐ no

5. You use the following transition words and phrases:

6. What I like best about your narrative is the following:

7. I recommend you make the following changes:

Proofreading Practice: Past Tense

Verb Tenses in Writing: Some Guidelines

1. Stay in the same tense as long as the time you are writing about does not change.

2. If the time changes, the verb tense *should* change, even in the same paragraph or sentence.

   Example: I once <u>believed</u> that money <u>makes</u> people happy, but now I <u>realize</u> that I <u>was</u> wrong.

3. Tell about the plot of a play, novel, or story in the *present tense*.

4. Statements about eternal truths may be in the present even when you are telling about past events:

   The child <u>learned</u> quickly that not all people in this world <u>can be trusted</u>.

5. If you are writing about experiences that you remember, statements such as "I recall" or "I remember" are in the present. The events happened in the past, but you are recalling them now:

I <u>remember</u> (not <u>remembered</u>) how hot the summers used to be in Arizona when I <u>was</u> a child.

In narrative writing, most of your sentences will be in the past tense. In the **past tense**, verbs fall into two categories: **regular verbs, which take *d*-endings**, and **irregular verbs, which change their spelling and do not take *d*-endings.**

Past Tense of Regular Verbs	Past Tense of Irregular Verbs
succeed<u>ed</u>	became
walk<u>ed</u>	bought
kiss<u>ed</u>	saw
stamped<u>ed</u>	drank
murder<u>ed</u>	sang
worshipp<u>ed</u>	took
doubt<u>ed</u>	drove
discuss<u>ed</u>	broke
wander<u>ed</u>	spent

D-Endings in the Past Tense

One of the most common writing errors is dropping or forgetting to add ***d*-endings** on regular verbs. Be careful to edit for *d*-endings when writing in the past tense.

When *Not* to Use *d*-Endings If you tend to omit *d*-endings in the past tense and are trying to check for missing *d*-endings in your final draft, remember that there are a few places where *d*-endings should *not* be used.

Do not use *d*-endings after *did* or *to*:

<u>Did</u> you <u>discuss</u> (not *discussed*) the salary?

They tried <u>to reach</u> (not *to reached*) the exit.

Do not use *d*-endings after other helping verbs such as *may*, *might, can, could, would, must,* and *should*:

She <u>might like</u> (not *liked*) to participate on the panel.

He <u>could learn</u> (not *learned*) a lot from you.

The Past Tense of Irregular Verbs

Irregular verbs never take *d*-endings. Instead, they change in different ways—*go* changes to *went, think* to *thought,* and so on. Most of these verbs you know by habit, but some cause frequent mistakes. Look over this list to see whether you recognize the past tenses.

Present	Past	Present	Past
be (am, is, are)	was, were	make	made
become	became	meet	met
begin	began	pay	paid
bring	brought	put	put
buy	bought	quit	quit
choose	chose	rise	rose
cost	cost	seek	sought
do	did	sell	sold
cut	cut	send	sent
feel	felt	shine	shone
fly	flew	sing	sang
get	got	spend	spent
give	gave	stand	stood
go	went	steal	stole
have	had	swim	swam
hear	heard	take	took
keep	kept	teach	taught
know	knew	tear	tore
lay	laid	think	thought
lead	led	throw	threw
lie	lay	write	wrote
lose	lost		

Proofreading Exercises: Basic, Intermediate, Challenge

☐ Basic Exercise: Past Tense

Find and correct the seven errors in the use of the past tense in the passage below:

> Last year when Ella was 15 she notice that her 11-year-old brother James was acting in a peculiar way. He was always going out for short walks all the time, and he would get angry if anybody ask him why he went out. At first she believe he was starting to hang with a gang and would get into trouble, but he spend too much time at home for that to happen. Once when she was coming home she saw him smoking a cigarette across the street from their house. He didn't see her watching him while he snuff out the cigarette butt before he went back inside. Ella was not happy to realized that he was developing a nicotine habit, but she feel a little relieved that he wasn't doing something worse.

◼ Intermediate Exercise: Past Tense

Find and correct the seven errors in the use of the past tense in the passage below:

> A tropical storm began forming out in the central Atlantic Ocean. Soon it gather strength and headed toward the Caribbean Islands. People in Haiti and the Dominican Republic start to board up their windows and to move their belongings into the safest shelters they could find. Soon, however, the storm changed direction and turn toward the coast of Florida, where people try to evacuate the coastal areas as meteorologists predict 120-mile-an-hour winds by the next morning. Fortunately, the winds subside somewhat and many of the residents along the coast escape serious damage to their homes, and few people were injured.

◼ Challenge Exercise: Past Tense

Find and correct the seven errors in the use of the past tense in the passage below:

> The psychologist Abraham Maslow did much to change our views of human nature. He began as an experimenter who spend most

of his time studying emotional illness. He wrote a book on abnormal psychology but then become dissatisfied with approaches that analyzed only disturbed persons. Instead, he choose to examine the characteristics of the unusually healthy person. He contribute significantly to modern psychology and brought a new emphasis on health and potential rather than sickness. He realize that many mysteries are still unsolved in the psychology of the healthy personality. He teach for many years and was a popular professor at several universities. Certain of his concepts, such as self-actualization and the hierarchy of needs, take their place among the leading ideas of modern psychology.

CHAPTER 8

ENUMERATING EXAMPLES

One of the simplest and best ways to develop ideas in an essay is to provide a series of examples to illustrate the point you are making. Generally, this means writing a paragraph, perhaps two, on each example, with an introductory and concluding paragraph tying them together. It is easy to organize an essay of this type, but it is not as easy to make it interesting: You must use creativity to produce a lively essay instead of a mechanical list. Try to write a thought-provoking introduction, make transitions between your paragraphs, and choose examples that are sufficiently different from one another to avoid repetition.

Student Essay: Enumerating Examples

Read the essay below and answer the questions that follow.

International Students Upgrade American Colleges

Reginald Stevens

One of the main reasons people come to the United States is to receive a college education which they can't get in their own countries. Some Americans may think that these foreign students are occupying places that

should be taken by students born in the U.S., and sometimes they make remarks about foreign students who
have trouble with English. What they should realize is
how much better American colleges are because of international students. *A few examples of students I know
would convince anybody that international students
improve the quality of colleges in the United States.*

**Thesis
Statement**

One of my friends is Carlton, a sophomore student
from my country of Guyana. Carlton is studying to be
a lawyer and wants to start his own practice in my country, where he hopes to enter politics someday. He is an
honors student and has been on the dean's list every one
of his four semesters. In most classes he does more work
than anybody else, and he helps other students after class
when they don't understand the lesson. Some people say
he is a politician already, and he is thinking about running for student government because he has been a
leader of the debate team, and after every debate someone comes up and tells him he should be in politics.

First Example

Another international student who contributes a
lot to my college is May, a student I met in chemistry
class. She will be graduating next semester and is
applying to veterinary schools. Her family comes from
South Korea, and she has been in this country for just
five years, but she speaks English really well, and she
won a creative writing prize for a short story she wrote.
May wants to stay in the United States. Her dream is to
move to California and have her own veterinary practice,
where she can care for rare animals that are becoming
extinct. She organized a group of students to travel to the
Galapagos Islands to study unusual species, and she was
the president of a club for students interested in pro-
tecting the environment. As a senior project she helped
the science department create a new course in ecology.

**Second
Example**

An even better example I know of an international
student who has contributed to the betterment of our
college is my friend and classmate Natasha. She spent
one year in a technical college in Moscow, and then her
family moved to the United States. Like many other
foreign students, she had to learn English in a hurry to

Final Example

continue her college education. In fact, her first semester she took only an ESL class and an advanced course in Russian literature. But after a year, she began to speak and write English well enough to earn high grades in all her courses. She is an outstanding pianist and has been the accompanist for the glee club since her second semester. She joins as many activities as she can and still does all her academic work. She helps the theater club with music and set design and has played three outstanding roles in school performances. Recently she was accepted into one of the best graduate theater programs to study directing. What makes her unique is that she not only added a lot to the school as a student, but she wants to come back some day and teach in the theater department after she makes a name for herself as a director.

Conclusion

It is true that international students like these compete with American students for admission to colleges, but there is a place somewhere for any qualified student. They also compete for grades with other students, but that is good because it gives American students more incentive. Coming from other cultures, international students bring experiences and knowledge that can enrich the educational experience of their classmates. Many of them also stay in the United States and contribute to our society after they graduate. Colleges should welcome more students from abroad.

1. Identify the sentence that best sums up the thesis of this essay.
2. What opposing opinion does Reginald mention and respond to?
3. What do all three of his examples have in common?
4. What differences are there among them?
5. How is the concluding paragraph linked to the introduction?
6. What transition words does he use at the beginning of the third and fourth paragraphs?
7. How well does your experience match the examples in this essay?

Example by a Published Author: Enumerating Examples

Endangered Habitats
Edward O. Wilson

The cutting of primeval forest and other disasters, fueled by the demands of growing human populations, are the overriding threat to biological diversity everywhere. . . .

Not many habitats in the world covering a kilometer contain fewer than a thousand species of plants and animals. Patches of rain forest and coral reef harbor tens of thousands of species, even after they have declined to a remnant of the original wilderness. But when the *entire* habitat is destroyed, almost all of the species are destroyed. . . . And so to threatened and endangered species must be added a growing list of ecosystems, comprising masses of species. Here are several deserving immediate attention:

Usambara Mountain forests, Tanzania. Varying widely in elevation and rainfall, the Usambaras contain one of the richest biological communities in East Africa. They protect large numbers of plant and animal species found nowhere else, but their forest cover is declining drastically, having already been cut to half, some 450 square kilometers, between 1954 and 1978. Rapid growth of human populations, more extensive logging, and the takeover of land for agriculture are pressing the last remaining reserves and thousands of species toward extinction.

San Bruno Mountain, California. In this small refuge surrounded by the San Francisco metropolis live a number of federally protected vertebrates, plants, and insects. Some of the species are endemics of the San Francisco peninsula, including the San Bruno elfin butterfly and the San Francisco garter snake. The native fauna and flora are threatened by offroad vehicular traffic, expansion of a quarry, and invasion by eucalyptus, gorse, and other alien plant species. . . .

The Colombian Chocó. The forest of Colombia's coastal plain and low mountains extends the entire length of the country. The Chocó, as the region is called after the state it includes, is drenched with extreme rainfall and blessed with one of the richest but least explored floras in the world. At present, 3,500 plant species are known but as many as 10,000 may grow there, of which one fourth are estimated to be endemic and a smaller but still substantial fraction are new to science. Since the early 1970s, the Chocó has been relentlessly invaded by timber companies and, to a lesser extent, by poor Colombians hungry for land. The forests are already down to about three quarters of their original cover and are being destroyed at an accelerating rate. . . .

But the long-term danger from climatic change looms in the decades ahead, for most ecosystems. If even the more modest projections of global warming prove correct, the world's fauna and flora will be trapped in a vise. On one side they are being swiftly reduced by deforestation and other forms of direct habitat destruction. On the other side they are threatened by the greenhouse effect.

—Edward O. Wilson. From *The Diversity of Life.*

1. Explain or look up the meaning of these words: ecosystems, vertebrates, endemics, fauna, flora, global warming, greenhouse effect.
2. What is Wilson warning us about in all of these examples?
3. What do all three examples have in common?
4. What differences do you notice?
5. What processes does he describe taking place in these regions?
6. In his book, Wilson actually lists 18 places in the world where ecosystems are in danger. Why does he list 18 instead of giving just one or two examples?
7. What conclusions can you draw from these examples?

WRITING TIP #8

Keeping your points in order by numbering them helps you and the reader follow your organizational plan. However, if you call too much attention to your essay's structure, it may seem mechanical and pedantic. It is usually better to avoid numbering your paragraphs by using the words *first, second,* and *third.* Do that in your early drafts; but bury the numbers in your final draft, using more attractive transitional words such as *another, next, further,* and *finally.* Be clear about your priorities: if you want to overwhelm the readers with the extent of a problem, give many examples. On the other hand, if your main purpose is to put across a simple point, use a few brief but convincing examples.

Writing Exercises: Basic, Intermediate, Challenge

☐ Basic Exercise: Illustration by Examples

Write an essay giving three or four examples of activities you like to do in your spare time. Use at least a paragraph to explain why you find each activity satisfying. Create transitions between paragraphs so that the essay doesn't read like a laundry list of items. Do a prewriting activity in order to identify a main point about your spare time activities, such as, "For me, my hobbies are more important than my job" or "All of my spare-time activities are closely related to my career goals."

☐ Intermediate Exercise: Illustration by Examples

Write an essay giving three or four examples of people who achieved success by overcoming handicaps. These may be famous people or acquaintances of yours. Remember that there are many kinds of handicaps, so your essay should tie your examples together around a clear main point. For example, you could argue that people are sometimes challenged to succeed in the very area in which they experience a disability (such as a person with a speech handicap who becomes an actor), or you could develop the idea that people who overcome handicaps inspire us all to have the courage to face our own difficulties.

■ Challenge Exercise: Illustration by Examples

Write an essay in which you give three or four examples of bias in the media. Explain how several newspapers, news magazines, or news programs on television or radio appear to you to slant the news in a particular way. Tie your essay together by making a point about how this kind of biased reporting can be recognized by the public. Before writing your first draft, spend some time looking over some news reports and watching or listening to programs that claim to be unbiased. Concentrate on three or four of these particular programs or articles, preferably on the same or similar topics.

Essay Topics: Illustration by Examples

1. Give three or four examples of films that send important messages.
2. Give three or four examples of athletes who made surprising comebacks.
3. Give three or four examples of violent television programs.
4. Give three or four examples of jobs once called "men's jobs" now done by women.
5. Give three or four examples of vacation sites that are particularly good for children.
6. Give three or four examples of athletic activities that are good for older people.
7. Give three or four examples of work that people do at home.

PEER REVIEW QUESTIONS: ENUMERATION

1. Here is my impression of what you are illustrating in your essay:
2. Your introduction is interesting. ☐ yes ☐ no
   Your introduction makes the purpose of your essay clear.
   ☐ yes ☐ no
   The sentence that most nearly expresses your main point is the following:
3. You offer the following three or four examples to support your point:
4. You use the following transitional words and phrases to connect your examples:
5. Your conclusion (is/is not) effective for the following reason:
6. What I like best about your essay is the following:
7. I recommend you make the following changes:

Proofreading Practice: Parallel Structure

Enumeration involves seeing parallel situations and writing parallel statements. Add rhythm to your writing occasionally by using parallel structure. In his famous Gettysburg Address, Abraham Lincoln turned a speech that might have been forgotten into a document for the ages by giving it poetic rhythm. He did this primarily by using two- and three-part parallel combinations of words and phrases. Here, for example, is a passage based on such parallel combinations:

Fourscore and seven years ago our fathers brought forth on this continent, a new nation, <u>conceived in Liberty, and dedicated to the proposition</u> that all men are created equal.
    Now we are engaged in a great civil war, testing whether <u>that nation or any nation so conceived and so dedicated,</u> can long endure. We are met on a great battlefield of that war. We have come to dedicate a portion of that field, as a final resting place to those who

here gave their lives that that nation might live. It is altogether <u>fitting and proper</u> that we should do this.

But, in a larger sense, <u>we cannot dedicate—we cannot consecrate—we cannot hallow</u>—this ground. The brave men, <u>living and dead</u>, who struggled here, have consecrated it, far above our poor power to <u>add or detract</u>.

—Abraham Lincoln. From "The Gettysburg Address."

Notice that in each of the underlined combinations the words are in the same form: two verbs ("add or detract"), two adjectives ("fitting and proper"), and so on. Imagine how awkward the speech would be if it read, "We cannot dedicate, we cannot consecrate, to hallow is impossible. . . ." In using parallel form, Lincoln was careful to match all of the parts smoothly.

Sentences that contain two, three, or more elements in a series require parallel structure. Parallelism refers to the **forms** of the words, not their meaning. Do not try to match parts that do not fit:

| | adj | adj | | adj |
Incorrect: My sister is nosy, competitive, stuck up, and <u>never</u>

verb
<u>lends me any money</u>.

Be sure that all elements fit:

| | adj | adj | adj | adj |
Correct: My sister is nosy, competitive, stuck up, and <u>stingy</u>.

Or, if one element does not fit, you can take it out and put it in a separate sentence:

Also Correct: My sister is nosy, competitive, and stuck up. <u>Besides that, she never lends me any money.</u>

TEST YOURSELF: PARALLELISM

Rewrite each sentence so that the parallel series is correct. One sentence is correct.

1. My friend Jessica looks good in everything she wears: formal dresses, pants, swimsuits, and even wearing old clothes from the flea market.

2. There are several things you should do during a fire: stay out of elevators, all doors closed, call the fire department, and do not panic.

3. The story tells about a young woman who is oppressed by her father, her boss harasses her, but paralyzed by her fear of leaving home.

4. Registering for college courses takes a lot of persistence, patient, and resourcefulness.

5. The United States benefits from immigrants because they take jobs others do not want, bring strong family values to American society, and an increased percentage of young people in an aging society.

6. In the emergency room Thomas saw patients waiting, EMT workers rushing in with patients on gurneys, and office assistants helping patients fill out forms.

7. The school requires that all children wear uniforms, arrive punctually, do their homework, and good behavior at all times.

Answers: 1. and even old clothes from the flea market 2. keep all doors closed 3. harassed by her boss 4. patience 5. and increase the percentage 6. correct 7. and behave well at all times

Proofreading Exercises: Basic, Intermediate, Challenge

☐ Basic Exercise: Parallelism

Proofread the sentences below, underlining the words or phrases that do not match. Explain how they can be corrected to make them fit into parallel combinations.

1. Frank is lazy, resentful, and impatience.

2. The course stimulated my interest, gave me new ideas, and expanding my awareness.

3. Sports utility vehicles are durable in rugged terrain, convenient for camping, but they are wasteful on fuel.

4. Sam needs either a new job or he should get a raise.

5. To excel on this test, you should memorize the chapter headings, do all the exercises, and careful notes.

6. The surgeon worked carefully, swiftly, and professional.

7. Without money, brains, or untalented, he managed to succeed.

■ Intermediate Exercise: Parallelism

Write words or phrases in the blanks provided, being careful to match them with the other elments in the group.

> Charlene knew she had many qualifications for the job. She was experienced, efficient, and _____. Her previous employer gave her a letter of recommendation that stated how well she shared tasks with others, came up with new ideas for the firm, and _____. Nevertheless, as the day came for the interview, she felt hesitant and _____. She realized that an unattractive mannerism, a careless gesture, or _____ might create a bad impression. So many others must be seeking this job, she thought, that only the most _____ and knowledgeable candidates would be taken seriously. After spending an afternoon researching the company and _____, she felt more confident. Three years ago, when she took her last interview, she was poised, _____, and confident, so she knew she could succeed this time as well.

■ Challenge Exercise: Parallelism

Correct the underlined words or phrases to make them match the rest of the sentence in parallel combinations.

> Members of the state legislature decided to do something to reduce the number of traffic accidents in the state. They attributed the increased number of accidents to speeding, poorly maintained highways, and <u>there are drunken drivers</u>. Most of the legislators believed that more could be done to reduce traffic deaths and <u>why there are so many injuries</u> from accidents. Some members of the assembly believed that either more state police or <u>by enforcing current laws better</u> would help. However, others argued that passing new laws would help more than <u>to enforce current laws more strictly</u>. Some younger legislators pointed out some new problems. For example, they said that drivers were causing accidents when they used their cell phones to carry on conversations, read voice

messages, and <u>business deals</u>. These representatives proposed laws to prohibit the use of cell phones while driving, set severe penalties for drivers who cause accidents while using cell phones, and <u>creating</u> a publicity campaign to warn against the dangers of using cell phones while driving. A few members blamed older drivers for the problem and even proposed that the legislature deny seniors the right to drive, but they were interrupted, laughed at, and <u>members of the other party silenced them</u>.

CHAPTER 9
DEFINING A TERM

Dictionaries give us short definitions of a word when we are not sure of its meaning. Thesauruses, as well as essays, articles, and other books that define terms, do much more than that: they explain terms in greater depth for people who are already familiar with them. These additional reference materials help readers understand the concept embodied by a term from many perspectives. These sources really explain ideas, rather than simply clarifying the meaning of a word.

For this reason, it is not usually effective, though it may be tempting, to begin a definition essay with a quotation from a dictionary. Doing so is the least original way to begin such an essay, in part because that beginning can be a dead end rather than a springboard to inspiration. If you decide to start your essay that way, be sure to explain to your reader that a dictionary definition alone is not adequate information to help us understand a term fully. In addition, you provide your own short definition of the word as a foundation for building a broader explanation of the concept the word symbolizes.

Student Essay: Defining a Term

The Meaning of Friendship

Jocelyn Harkins

Most of us use the word *friendship* every day without thinking about what it really means. To many people, being a friend means only that two people spend time together, hang out at the same places, and get to know each other. But my definition of friendship is of two people deciding that they will be closely involved in each other's lives and support each other permanently, just like members of the same family. Sometimes they are more than family.

By my definition, many people who are called friends are just acquaintances. Relationships like that are convenient for a while until one of the people involved transfers to another college or moves to another city. Then they write to each other for a while until they forget about it. In other cases, people keep up long-term connections by writing or e-mailing but never really do anything to support each other or talk about what is really bothering them. Some people also consider their co-workers friends but forget that they see them only at work and don't know much about their personal lives. If one of them changes jobs, that's the end of their "friendship."

These kinds of relationships can't compare to a true friendship, which is based on a really close and supportive connection over many years, no matter if one of the parties moves away, changes jobs, or drops out of college. Real friends are there for each other, especially when they need each other because one of them is in the hospital or has a personal problem. In a poem called "The Death of the Hired Man" by Robert Frost, a homeless man who used to work for a couple on their farm is dying and he comes back to them. He doesn't have a home, but the wife says to her husband, "Home is the place where, when you have to go there,/They have to take you in." That's just the way a friend is: a person who will listen to you or help you when there is nobody else. To use computer language, a friend is the "default" person who can always be counted on and will always take you in.

One example in my life of a real friend is Sonya. We first met in middle school and became close friends. Then we went to the same high school for one year until she moved to Pittsburgh. We stayed in touch and visited each other for the next two years, and went to different colleges. I know we will continue to be friends for the rest of our lives, because we have stayed close even through experiences with boyfriends that didn't work out, changing jobs and going to different schools. I know we will be at each other's wedding and will be there if we have children and when either one of us has problems.

Using my definition, I would have to say there aren't many examples of true friends in the world. But everybody needs one or two true friends. Most people have a lot of co-workers, family members, and acquaintances, but sometimes they don't serve our needs like a true friend. Many families are dysfunctional and not supportive, and we can't count on acquaintances and co-workers to be there next year or the year after when we need them. Nothing can take the place of a true friend.

1. In your own words, explain what Jocelyn means by a true friend.
2. Identify the kinds of relationships she considers not true friendship.
3. Identify the thesis statement in this essay.
4. What is the difference in purpose between paragraphs 2 and 3?
5. What is the purpose of her quotation from Robert Frost's poem in paragraph 3?
6. What method does Jocelyn use to develop paragraph 4?
7. What opinions does Jocelyn express that might be explored and debated further?

Example by a Published Author: Definition Essay

Read the following passage defining the term *community* and answer the questions that follow.

A Sociologist Defines the Term "Community"
Amitai Etzioni

A key concept I draw upon in the following characterization of a good society is the term "community." Given that it has been repeatedly argued that such a social entity cannot be defined, this matter is first addressed. Several critics have argued that the concept of community is so ill-defined that it has no identifiable designation. Robert Booth Fowler, in his book, *The Dance with Community*, shows that the term is used in six different and rather incompatible ways.[1] Colin Bell and Howard Newby write, "There has never been a theory of community, nor even a satisfactory definition of what community is."[2] In another text, Bell and Newby write, "But what is community? . . . It will be seen that over ninety definitions of community have been analyzed and that the one common element in them all was man!"[3] Margaret Stacey argues that the solution to this problem is to avoid the term altogether.[4]

As I see it, this "cannot be defined" is a tired gambit. We have difficulties in precisely defining even such a simple concept as a chair. Something to sit on? One can sit on a bench or bed. Something to sit on with four legs? Many chairs have three, or even just one, and so on. The same criticism has been leveled against rationality, democracy, and class, and yet nobody seriously suggests we stop using these concepts.

The following definition seems to me quite workable: "Community is a combination of two elements: (a) A web of affect-laden relationships among a group of individuals, relationships that often criss-cross and reinforce one another (rather than merely one-on-one or chainlike individual relationships). (b) A measure of commitment to a set of shared values, norms, and meanings, and a shared history and identity—in short, to a particular culture."[5]

The definition leaves open the amount of conflict that occurs within a given community, but does define it as a social entity that has the elements necessary (bonds and shared values) to contain conflict within sustainable boundaries. Moreover, the definition indicates

---

[1]Robert Booth Fowler, *The Dance with Community* (Lawrence: University Press of Kansas, 1991), 142.
[2]Colin Bell and Howard Newby, *The Sociology of Community: A Selection of Readings* (London: Frank Cass, 1974), xiii.
[3]Colin Bell and Howard Newby, *Community Studies: An Introduction to the Sociology of the Local Community* (New York: Praeger, 1973), 15.
[4]Cited in Bell and Newby, *Community Studies*, 49.
[5]Amitai Etzioni, *The New Golden Rule: Community and Morality in a Democratic Society* (New York: Basic Books, 1996), 127.

that communities need not be territorial. Indeed, there are many ethnic, professional, gay, and other communities that are geographically dispersed; that is, the members of these communities reside among people who are not members. (Often, these communities are centered around particular institutions, such as places of worship, hiring halls, bars, or social clubs.)

—Amitai Etzioni. From *The Monochrome Society*.

1. Define or look up the following words: *entity, incompatible, gambit, affect-laden*.

2. According to Etzioni, are there a few, or many, definitions that have been offered for the word *community*? Do the sources he cites agree or disagree about the number of definitions that have been given?

3. What other common words does he mention that are difficult to define?

4. In your own words, explain the two parts of Etzioni's definition of *community*.

5. Does Etzioni believe that conflict can occur within a community without destroying its identity as a community?

6. What does he mean when he says that communities "need not be territorial"?

7. What examples does he give of communities that are not territorial? Give an example of one community that is territorial and one that is not.

Examples of Short Definitions

Here are three short definitions of terms that might be used to develop larger definitions of the accompanying concepts in the form of essays:

Attention Deficit Disorder (ADD) is a neurological disorder that causes people to have difficulty focusing on sustained tasks.

String theory is a recent concept in physics that seeks to unify the four basic forces in the cosmos by explaining the behavior of particles much smaller than electrons.

Graphic novels are works of fiction designed in the form of cartoons but, unlike comic books, with realistic characters and serious plots.

You may be expected to write a definition essay on familiar concepts such as *success, love, democracy, maturity, responsibility, courage, mother, father, liberty,* and so on. It is possible to compose original essays on such subjects, even though they have been written about for centuries. If you take on one of these topics, however, you will have to limit its scope. Instead of writing about love in general, for instance, you would probably do better to write about a specific type of love—romantic love, love for one's country, love of God, or love of humanity—and find your own way of defining it.

Limiting the Scope of Your Definition

Such broad topics must be focused before you write. *Success,* for example, is too large a topic for a cohesive essay if you do not limit it in some way. This may mean concentrating on your individual definition of success. For instance, to define *success* effectively, you might want to explain what success is *not,* i.e., what people sometimes mistakenly think it means. Everything in your essay should then focus on and back up your unique definition without wandering off this purpose.

Examining Your Subject from Different Angles

Try doing a cubing exercise to explore the range of a broad topic. For discussion, let's stick with the term *success* as a subject for a definition essay. How can you describe success; to what can you compare it? What is it associated with? Can you analyze its causes and effects and divide it into parts? How is success used in the world? What can you say for or against striving for success? Try cubing or focused writing to gather perspectives on success.

Obviously, you will have a lot to say, and there are plenty of examples of success you can include in your essay.

Giving Examples of the Concept

Let's say you have come up with an original definition of *success* that will allow you to create an effective essay. You have decided that *success* is getting the most out of every experience and learning from it, whether the experience is a victory or defeat, a triumph or disappointment. One of the best ways to make your essay believable and interesting is to think of several real-life examples of such success. Maybe you know a friend who kept failing in school and at work but ultimately succeeded by learning from his failures. Perhaps you could give an example from history of a person who, like Abraham Lincoln, failed many times but learned from his setbacks. Or perhaps you could mention Maya Angelou or another writer who used all she learned from her difficult experiences to compose meaningful books that positively influenced others.

> ### WRITING TIP #9
> In creating definitions, try to avoid the **"is when"** error. It is ungrammatical to write, "Success <u>is when</u> you reach an important goal." *Success* is a noun and should not be equated with a *when* clause: "when you reach an important goal" tells *when* something happened, not *what* something is. It is grammatically preferable to write, "Success is <u>the achievement</u> of an important goal" or "Success means <u>reaching</u> an important goal." You may also write, "A person succeeds <u>when</u> he or she reaches an important goal."

Correct these two sentences:

Wealth is when you have a lot of money.

Arbitration is when a third party is brought in to settle a dispute.

Writing Exercises: Basic, Intermediate, Challenge

☐ Basic Exercise: Definition Essays

Respond to the following:

1. Write a sentence giving your own definition of the term *hero*.
2. Identify two kinds of heroism.
3. Describe what you think is a false notion of heroism.
4. Name two people who fit your definition of a hero.
5. In one sentence, explain why people admire heroes.
6. In one sentence, explain one good effect of heroes.
7. In one sentence, identify one kind of harm heroes can do.

▮ Intermediate Exercise: Definition Essays

Choose one of the following terms and respond to the instructions:

love   courage   happiness   faith   beauty   intelligence

1. Write one sentence in which you give your definition of one of these terms.
2. Identify at least three types of this concept.
3. Identify two people who exemplify this concept, one whom you know from personal experience and one who is a public personality.
4. Identify one familiar definition of this term that you reject in favor of your own definition.
5. Describe the causes or effects of this concept.
6. Explain what this concept is associated with.
7. Explain what is the opposite of this concept.

▮ Challenge Exercise: Definition Essays

Choose one of the following terms and respond to the instructions:

philosophy   economics   literature   science   art   psychology

1. Write one sentence in which you give your definition of one of these terms.

2. Identify at least three types of this concept.

3. Identify two examples of this concept, one from personal experience and one from a public personality.

4. Identify one familiar definition of this term that you reject in favor of your own definition.

5. Identify the goals and objectives of this field of knowledge.

6. Explain what benefits one gains from knowing about this discipline.

7. Explain what is the opposite of this concept.

Essay Topics: Definition

Write an essay based on one of the exercises above, <u>or:</u>

1. Find three dictionary definitions of *morality* and write an essay in which you analyze these definitions and develop one of your own. Explain how people acquire their notions of moral and immoral behavior, and explain whether concepts of good and evil are the same everywhere or vary from one society to another and one person to another. Include examples of people whose lives demonstrate moral or immoral behavior.

2. Write an essay defining the word *adult*. Explain what it means to be a grown-up in attitudes, values, priorities, and behavior. Include several examples of mature and immature behavior, as well as examples of several people who you think are grown-up and several who you think are not.

3. Write an essay defining the term *addiction*. Explain how a mere habit or preference for something becomes an addiction and the difference between a habit and an addiction. Include examples of addictive behavior and of different things people become addicted to.

4. Define the term *hip-hop*. Describe the music itself as well as the culture and attitudes surrounding it. Explain how the hip-hop culture developed and how it differs from previous popular music culture. Give examples of several hip-hop artists and explain why they are popular.

5. Write an essay defining *entertainment*. Explain the difference between entertainment and education, religion, politics, and

journalism—all of which sometimes contain elements of entertainment. Give examples of some of these categories, showing the difference between pure entertainment and education, religion, etc.

6. Write an essay defining the term *pornography*. Explain the difference between pornography and genuine art, literature, film, theater, or research that contains sex and violence. Give examples of pornography and of art that contains these elements.

7. Find several definitions of the word *democracy* in dictionaries or political science textbooks. Write an essay in which you develop your own definition of the word and explain how well the political structures of several countries, including the United States, do or do not match your definition.

PEER REVIEW QUESTIONS: DEFINITION

1. I think that your overall intention in this essay is to define the term _____ so that we understand the following about it:

2. Your introduction is interesting. ☐ yes ☐ no
   Your introduction identifies the term you are defining.
   ☐ yes ☐ no
   The sentence that most nearly states your definition of the term is the following:

3. You develop your definition by the following method:

4. You give the following examples of the concept you are defining:

5. Your conclusion (is/is not) effective for the following reason:

6. What I like best about your essay is the following:

7. I recommend you make the following changes:

Proofreading Practice: Use of Pronouns; *Who* and *Which* Clauses

Personal pronouns are the words such as *I, you, he, she, it, we,* and *they* that take the place of nouns. Using pronouns correctly means choosing the right **case** of the pronoun. When the pronoun is the subject of a statement, use **I, he, she, we,** and **they**; when the pronoun is the object of a verb or preposition, use **me, him, her, us,** and **them**:

She and I met them in the hallway.

They knew what would happen to him, and we knew it too.

Notice that *it* and *you* have the same form in both subject and object position:

You will hear it when it comes closer to you.

Common mistakes occur most often when pronouns are used in combination:

Incorrect: Me and him went to the same high school.

Correct: He and I went to the same high school.

Incorrect: Between you and I there should not be any secrets.

Correct: Between you and me there should be no secrets.

In informal speech, we also hear statements such as this:

Informal: Me and my friends have been doing yoga for six months.

Standard: My friends and I have been doing yoga for six months.

If such combinations confuse you and you are not sure whether to use *I* or *me, we* or *us, he* or *him, she* or *her, they* or *them,* eliminate one of the pronouns and read the sentence with only one. You will almost always know which is right:

Me and my friends often study in the cafeteria.

Eliminate "my friends": You would not write, "Me often study in the cafeteria."

Correct: <u>My friends and I</u> like to study in the cafeteria.

Relative pronouns—*who*, *which*, and *that*—introduce **relative clauses**, which are often used in definition essays. A clause beginning with *who*, *which*, or *that* is called a *relative clause* because it is *related* to some person or thing preceding it. Take, for example, this sentence:

> The Cooperative Education Department has arranged an internship for Melissa, <u>who wants experience in a publishing firm</u>.

The relative clause in this sentence gives useful information about Melissa relating to her desire for an internship. Because this clause only relates to the main clause, it will not stand alone as a whole sentence. One error to avoid is to leave a relative clause as a fragment by separating it from the main clause.

Avoiding Relative Clause Fragments

As a general rule, do not try to begin sentences with the words *who*, *which*, or *that*. These words usually begin relative clauses, not whole sentences. Doing so will almost certainly produce a fragment. The sentence above cannot be divided into two sentences:

Incorrect: The Cooperative Education Department has arranged

fragment

an internship for Melissa. <u>Who wants experience in a publishing firm.</u>

Incorrect: After completing the first part of the examination, students will have one hour to do the second part.

fragment

<u>Which will be given to them by the proctors.</u>

fragment

Incorrect: Samantha is excited about a Web site. <u>That she discovered while doing research on South American music.</u>

Another error that occurs frequently with relative clauses is the lack of agreement between verbs and the words they represent, called **antecedents**. In our first sentence, we have the clause *who wants experience in a publishing firm*. In this clause, the verb *wants* has an *s*-ending. We cannot tell whether it should be *who want* or *who wants* until we identify the antecedent, which is *Melissa*. If we change the sentence to plural, with two antecedents, Melissa and Hector, the verb changes:

Relative clause (plural): The Cooperative Education Department has arranged internships for Melissa and Hector, who <u>want</u> experience in publishing firms.

Restrictive and Nonrestrictive Clauses

Should you use a comma before *which* and *who*? Sometimes you should and sometimes you should not—it depends on whether the clause is **restrictive** or **nonrestrictive**. A **restrictive clause** is one that is necessary to the meaning of a sentence; a **nonrestrictive clause** is one that simply adds extra information to a sentence that can be understood without it. A nonrestrictive clause is a bit like a phrase you could put in parentheses—interesting, but not crucial. For instance, if I write, "William Jefferson Clinton, *who was in the White House from 1992 to 2000*," the *who* clause adds information that is not necessary for the reader to identify President Clinton. However, if I write, "presidents *who complete two terms in office*," the reader cannot identify which presidents I am referring to without including the *who* clause. Please note that clauses beginning with *that* are always restrictive; do not set them off with commas. Many stylists will also advise you to use *that* rather than *which* in restrictive clauses:

Preferred: The books <u>that you ordered</u> have arrived.

Acceptable: The books *which you ordered* have arrived.

Nonrestrictive Clause with Comma: Toni Morrison's *Sula*, which is on the reading list, has been ordered by the bookstore.

Using *Who* and *Whom*

Whether to use *who* or *whom* depends upon how the word is used within its clause, not upon the rest of the sentence. For instance, write, "Give it to the person *who* needs it." *Whom* would not work here, because *who* is the subject of the verb *needs*. However, it would be correct to write, "Give it to *whomever* you choose." In this sentence, *whomever* is the object of the verb *choose*. In reverse form, the clause reads, "You choose *whomever*." Notice that the beginnings of the two sentences are the same: "Give it to. . . ." The function of *who* or *whom* in its own clause, then, is what tells you which form to use, not what the rest of the sentence says.

TEST YOURSELF: PRONOUNS AND RELATIVE CLAUSES

Correct the error in each sentence. One sentence is already correct.

1. The class watched a film called *The Experience of Childbirth*. Which was informative but not entirely up to date.
2. The winner of the recount was the incumbent mayor. Who was expected to win by a wide margin.
3. Ted took all of the psychology courses that was offered by the college.
4. E-mail responses came back from all the students who the club invited.
5. Kimberly often consults her academic adviser, who have helped her apply to graduate school.
6. The company designed its Web site for the younger customers whom it wished to attract.
7. Most of the assignments, that Robert missed can still be made up.

Answers: 1. *Childbirth*, which 2. mayor, who 3. courses that were offered 4. whom the club 5. who has helped 6. correct 7. assignments that

Proofreading Exercises: Basic, Intermediate, Challenge

☐ Basic Exercise: Pronouns and Relative Clauses

Find the seven errors in this passage. Look for fragments, misuse or lack of commas, errors in verb forms, and wrong pronoun case.

To people like you and I, happiness means having your life the way you want it. Some people define happiness as just a feeling, that you have when you just had a wonderful meal or saw a great film. I prefer to define it as a situation. In which you have succeeded in arranging your personal life and your career in satisfying ways. Several things that is important to happiness are understanding your own needs, relating well to others, and setting realistic goals. Happiness can come to anyone, but it is most likely to be achieved by thoughtful persons. Who understand that they can reach many goals if they are willing to make the necessary sacrifices. In public life me and my friends see many examples of people, who have attained a level of happiness that we all might wish to attain.

◼ Intermediate Exercise: Pronouns and Relative Clauses

Find the seven errors in this passage. Look for fragments, misuse or lack of commas, errors in verb forms, and wrong pronoun case.

The word *democracy* is favored by most nations and is certainly important to we Americans. Many countries cannot truly be called democratic. A true democracy is a country, in which the government belongs to the people, not to a small elite group. Open and fair elections are necessary to any democracy. Elections that are free of corruption and control by rich and powerful groups or individuals. A system of checks and balances, which protects the integrity of the government and prevent one official or body from gaining absolute control, is also needed. A leader who the people legitimately elect will work within such a system better than a dictator. Who is accustomed to having no one question his opinions and orders. Although many countries have elements of democracy, none of them is likely to become a perfect democracy. Which is a utopian form of government not yet possible in the world of politics as we know it.

◼ Challenge Exercise: Pronouns and Relative Clauses

Write sentences of your own following these instructions:

1. Write a sentence beginning with a person's name followed by a comma and *who*.

2. Write a sentence beginning with the name of your college followed by a comma and *which*.

3. Write a sentence using the phrase *me and my classmates* correctly.

4. Write a sentence using the phrase *she and I* correctly.

5. Write a sentence using *that has* after a singular antecedent.

6. Write a sentence using *that have* after a plural antecedent.

7. Write a sentence using *whom* correctly.

STEP THREE

WRITING ESSAYS BASED ON YOUR READING AND RESEARCH

CHAPTER 10
MAKING A COMPARISON

Comparing and Contrasting as a Way of Knowing

Making comparisons is something we begin doing as children. It is a fundamental way of understanding our world, from the time we compare toys and favorite games as toddlers to the time we write comparative essays in college. Writing an insightful, well-organized comparison on any subject is a way of understanding the subject better. You will probably be asked to write comparison/contrast essays on term papers and exams, so it is a good idea to learn about this mode of composition.

Types of Comparison

Creating essays that compare people, places, experiences, or concepts is a challenge. It requires you to juggle language, content, and organization; therefore, you should learn to work with a clear plan. Above all, remember what a comparison is for: to understand your subject better. The best way to do that is to **discuss the subjects together**. Begin your essay with an introduction that mentions *both* persons or things, not just one. This way, you will avoid the trap of discussing one, then the other, and leaving the reader to figure out how the subjects are similar or different. Which of these two sentences makes a better starting point for a comparison?

1. Making a film is more complicated than making a CD album.
2. Making a film is very expensive.

Either sentence might make a good subject for an essay, but only Sentence 1 contains a comparison. We expect the writer to give several reasons why making films is more complicated than making CD albums. In the process, we expect to learn a lot about both filmmaking and music recording.

These are the three general types of comparison.

Categories of Comparison

Parallels: Pointing out similarities between two people or things

Contrasts: Pointing out differences between two people or things

Comparison/Contrast: Pointing out similarities and differences between two people or things

The following three paragraphs illustrate the three main kinds of comparison. The first paragraph discusses the similarities between two activities, the second contrasts the differences between two experiences, and the third explores the similarities and the differences between two U.S. presidents. Notice that all three passages begin with sentences that mention both subjects.

Paragraph A

Comparing two similar activities:

Thomas realized that his two favorite activities, reading and shopping, have a lot in common. First, he spends a lot of time doing both, even though both take a lot of effort. Sometimes when he shops, he drives to a large wholesale store where he has a membership, and he stocks up on a large number of supplies at low cost. He also has a membership in a bookstore chain and sometimes picks up a large number of books at once, and sometimes he checks out a lot of books from the school library at the same time. When he reads, he likes to browse through all these books and some magazines to pick out something that suits his mood, just as he browses in the supermarket to select something that suits his taste buds at the moment. He likes to compare favorite writers the way he compares groceries. In his reading, he tries to balance some informative, high quality selections with some that he reads for entertainment. Likewise, when he shops, he can't resist some junk food and cheap clothes just because he feels the impulse to buy them. These, too, he balances with purchases that show more long-range judgment. And in both shopping and reading, he alternates between short spurts of activity and multi-hour marathons of patient concentration. Thomas prides himself on being the best shopper and the best reader in his family.

Paragraph B
Contrasting two opposite experiences:

Wanda's experiences in high school and college were totally different. In the large urban high school she attended, she often felt overwhelmed by the crowds of students she didn't know, and she didn't have the confidence to join athletic teams or participate in extracurricular activities. She had the opportunity to choose from many available courses, but the classes were often crowded. In the small liberal arts college she attended, she felt more at home because she developed many friendships and joined the drama club. The small seminars encouraged her to be active in class, and even though she was now far away from home, she was able to adjust to the new environment with the help of a counselor. On the other hand, she sometimes missed the energy of the city and the variety of students around her in her high school.

Paragraph C
Comparing and contrasting two presidents:

Presidents William Jefferson Clinton and George W. Bush may resemble each other on the surface, but to their supporters they are very different. Both men were governors of Southern states before being elected president, and both speak with a slight Southern accent. Both were elected at a fairly young age and were more athletic than most political leaders. Both came from Protestant backgrounds and appealed to churchgoers. Both were first elected with less than 50% of the votes cast, and both had exhibited imperfect behavior in the past, which their supporters considered irrelevant but their opponents frequently criticized. However, these resemblances are superficial, and as their supporters will tell you, the two men represent entirely different political philosophies. President Clinton favored government policies to help the poor and a foreign policy based on negotiation, whereas President

Bush favored stimulating business through tax cuts and an aggressive foreign policy based on military action. President Clinton appointed mostly liberal judges, whereas President Bush appointed very conservative ones. Whatever similarities the public may have seen in their styles, they tried to point the country in very different directions.

As you might guess, there are not many pairs of things that are totally different or completely similar. Consequently, there are not many essays of the first two types, and you are more likely to be asked to write a comparison/contrast essay. This is a more interesting intellectual task, but also a more challenging one. It helps us see the complex nature of reality.

Gathering Facts on Both Subjects

Writing an interesting and meaningful comparison requires facts. Usually this means looking up information on the Web, reading books and magazines, or interviewing people who know a lot about your subject. Writers who succeed in their efforts to compare often have done a lot of research and preliminary thinking, and they start writing with a wealth of facts in front of them. To create a better comparison/contrast essay, begin by gathering your facts, concentrating on similarities and differences as you obtain information. Brainstorm to explore the range of facts you can assemble on each subject. Then do a cluster to identify the categories you are using to make the comparison. Following that, make lists of similarities and differences in each category. Your essay will be much richer as a result of this prewriting work.

Exploring Similarities and Differences: A Student Writer at Work

Andrea Johnson had to write a comparison essay. She decided to use the assignment as an opportunity to look into two careers she was considering—pediatric nursing and elementary education. Before writing her essay, Andrea gathered information on both careers, partly from what she and her friends already knew about both professions, and partly from reading, talking with relatives in both fields, and doing Web searches. Here is a list of similarities and differences she compiled, grouped into categories she wanted to know more about.

Andrea's Brainstorming Notes about Two Career Options

Nursing vs. Teaching: Preparation and Training

Similarities:

Both careers require college degrees and training on the job.

Requirements for both careers set by state and professional regulations that change frequently.

Some use of computer technology required in both.

Courses in child psychology also required in both.

High academic averages needed, and both nurses and teachers have to pass state licensing examinations that include specialized and general knowledge.

Differences:

Nursing training more specialized and technical—less general education.

Nurses in some states can practice with a two-year degree and an R.N., but teachers must have a bachelor's degree and many even have master's degrees.

Nurses required to update their technical knowledge in many states to be re-licensed. Teachers often expected to keep doing professional development but not so technical.

Teachers and nurses both have to use information technology, but teachers don't need advanced science unless they're science teachers.

Personal Characteristics Needed

Similarities:

Both careers involve working with children, so both take a lot of patience, energy, and caring.

Nurses and teachers both have to relate to all the children without bias and need plenty of insight into children's feelings. They also must be mature themselves so that they can help and guide children.

Differences:

Nurses mostly help children one at a time, must be good at one-on-one relationships with many kinds of children who have many kinds of physical problems. Teachers have to control and guide whole classrooms and project a strong personality and enough authority to teach many students at once.

Nurses often have to help children suffering from illness or pain, but teachers have to inspire and lead students mostly when they're healthy. Nurses have to be good in times of crisis and able to stay calm in emergencies. Teachers have to be able to create a positive group feeling and maintain a sense of purpose all day long as group leaders.

Teachers often earn tenure and stay at the same school in the same job for years, sometimes even for their whole career. Nurses often can change from one kind of job to another and from one kind of institution to another.

Pay and Opportunities

Similarities:

Both careers often pay good salaries and benefits but vary according to state and locality. Both careers offer opportunities for advancement, especially for those who get advanced certification or degrees.

Some administrative posts open in both fields.

Differences:

Nursing pays more at the beginning. Teachers can earn quite a lot in the long run, especially with advanced degrees.

Teachers may be able to become principals or superintendents with even higher salaries if they get further certification; nurses, however, can't become doctors or hospital administrators without extensive further education.

Teachers mostly work in schools; nurses work in many kinds of situations, including clinics, hospitals, and even schools.

Satisfactions and Difficulties

Similarities:

Both jobs require many hours of hard work and much repetition.

Both jobs offer security to experienced professionals because teachers can usually earn tenure and nurses are very much in demand. Both nurses and teachers usually feel that the work they do is very important and can sometimes make an enormous difference in children's lives.

Both nurses and teachers have to cope with children who are unruly or difficult.

Differences:

Teachers have two or three months off during summer vacation, whereas nurses work year round, with shorter vacations.

Teachers have tenure and nurses don't, but nurses can usually change jobs easily and find a new job if they lose one.

The satisfaction nurses get sometimes involves saving a child's life or restoring him or her to health. Teachers' satisfaction is more general, comes from knowing that you may have made a difference in the overall development of the child's knowledge and values.

Teachers work with students for whole semesters or whole years. Nurses sometimes see children once or twice to give them a shot or help them during a stay in the hospital and never see them again. Nurses may work with individual children for long periods of time if they have long-term illnesses or disabilities.

Teachers have to deal with behavioral problems of students in large groups; nurses have to cope with individual children when they refuse to take medicine, are afraid, or are uncooperative.

Organizing Your Material

Once Andrea gathered enough material to compose a successful, meaningful comparison, she was faced with the decision of how to organize it. Unlike narratives, comparisons do not organize themselves, so planning is crucial. At first, Andrea thought she would use the block pattern of organization, first writing about nursing, then writing about teaching. This is the easiest way to organize a comparison, and the one most writers fall back on if they do not plan ahead.

The Block Method of Organizing

1. Introduction
2. A body paragraph or two on the first subject (Nursing)
3. transition
4. A body paragraph or two on the second subject (Teaching)
5. transition
6. Several paragraphs analyzing similarities and differences between the subjects (Be sure to include this part)
7. Conclusion

The block method can be effective, and it looks easy. But inexperienced writers who use it often write two flimsily connected descriptions and leave it to the reader to analyze two subjects' similarities and differences. If you use the block form, keep both subjects in mind at all times, mentioning similarities and differences between them in every part of your essay. Begin your introduction by mentioning both topics, make a transition that clearly shows their connection, and continue with a full discussion of their similarities and differences. Remember that it is your job, as the writer, to analyze your topics' similarities and differences—do not leave the work to your reader.

The Similarities/Differences Method of Organization

Andrea considered two other possible patterns of organization. The second is to write first about all the similarities between the two subjects, then about the differences. An outline of this method would look something like the following:

1. Introduction
2. Several paragraphs discussing similarities between the two subjects (Nursing and Teaching)
3. transition
4. Several paragraphs discussing differences between the two subjects (Nursing and Teaching)
5. Conclusion

You can reverse this plan and discuss the differences first. Either method is effective when you want to show readers that what most people think about your two subjects is untrue. For example, let's say that your readers believe two presidents or two athletes are just alike. To address this perspective, discuss the similarities between the subjects first, but then use the rest of the essay to contrast them by showing that they are actually different. Or, you can surprise your readers by showing that two subjects that most people think of as widely different really have a lot in common. In that case, you discuss the differences first, and then the similarities.

Organizing by Categories

Andrea considered a third, more complicated type of comparison essay—the kind in which you provide a running analysis of similarities and differences by moving from one category to another, as Andrea did in her brainstorming. For instance, a comparison of stories might move from a discussion of settings to one of plots and then one of themes. This kind of essay may seem difficult at first, but it can result in impressive essays. (This is especially true when you use this method on an essay examination.)

Picture the method of organizing by categories as follows:

1. Introduction
2. A paragraph on the similarities/differences in category #1
3. transition
4. A paragraph on the similarities/differences in category #2

5. transition

6. A paragraph on the similarities/differences in category #3

7. Conclusion

Student Essay: Exploring Similarities and Differences

Andrea's brainstorming notes grouped her ideas into categories using the last method described above. During brainstorming, however, she decided that her thesis—the idea she wanted to argue about the two careers—would be stronger if she used a different method of organization than grouping by categories. Read her essay and identify which method of organization she used.

Becoming a Nurse or a Teacher
Andrea Johnson

What kind of person should become a nurse or a teacher? Most people probably think the same kind of person could be either one. But there are nurses who want to quit and become teachers and teachers with master's degrees who have entered nursing programs. Students who are considering becoming pediatric nurses or elementary school teachers should realize that these two professions, which used to be linked together in people's minds as "women's work," require different skills and different personalities. To outsiders, they may seem similar, but those on the inside know how different they are.

It's true that, superficially, nursing and teaching seem to have a lot in common. Pediatric nurses can save children's lives and restore them to health. Elementary teachers sometimes inspire children to great achievements and turn around lives that might have been thrown away. They both work with children every day, and they both need to know a lot about child psychology. They have to be caring, patient, and firm in the way they treat children, and they must have a sense of humor as well as the ability to see and appreciate all the differences between children of different backgrounds.

In addition to working with children, nurses and teachers both have to have a lot of education and must pass licensing tests to practice their profession. Nurses can have a two-year degree or a bachelor's degree, and some even have a master's or Ph.D. Teachers need at least a bachelor's degree, and in many states they have to earn a master's. Both jobs pay in the $40,000 to $60,000 range for people with experience, and both are pretty secure. Good teachers usually earn tenure after a number of years, and nurses are so much in demand that if they are well qualified they can almost always get a job. In both professions, however, nurses and teachers have to earn licenses by passing tests and may have to renew their licenses after several years. In many states this means taking additional courses or doing other kinds of professional development to keep up with current trends in the field.

Although people who choose nursing and teaching are usually not ambitious in the same sense that politicians and business executives are, both careers offer possibilities for advancement. Nursing has a number of specialties and administrative posts, and teachers can, with extra certification, become assistant principals or principals, or even superintendents, just as some nurses return to medical school and become doctors.

If these careers are so similar, wouldn't the same people be good at both? It turns out that if you talk to people inside these professions, they really aren't much alike. Both work with children, but nurses mostly see children one at a time, children who suffer illness or accidents, or have other health problems. Teachers have to manage whole classrooms of children, and they rarely have time to relate closely to individual children. That means that nurses and teachers need different skills and maybe even different personalities. Although both have to be caring and patient, teachers have to spend most of their day projecting a strong sense of authority, purpose, and direction so that all their students learn. They have to be good organizers and planners but do not have to be ready to face life-or-death emergencies, suffering, and even death. Nurses have to maintain empathy for all of the children they help, and they need a lot of skill in relating to children who are afraid or in pain. They can't be too sensitive about the sight of blood or broken bones, and they shouldn't expect to have much long-term impact on children's attitudes or values.

Although both jobs require hard work, teachers have summer vacations that last two or three months, while nurses have less time off. Nurses have to work year round, but they don't have to take home endless papers, exams, and lab reports to grade or to plan lessons. Teachers always work in schools, but nurses may work in hospitals, clinics, or even schools and take on a variety of responsibilities. This means that a teacher should be someone who can imagine herself or himself doing almost the same work for many years and who prefers stability, while a nurse may change from one kind of work to another or even from one kind of institution to another.

Teachers could be described as "long-term" people. The satisfactions they get usually come from knowing that they have made a difference in a child's life that may be evident years later. We've all heard of celebrities who attribute their success to an elementary teacher whom they never forgot. Nurses are more "high adrenalin" people who gain satisfaction from intervening in children's lives in ways that may save them from dying or restore them to health. They may not have to work as frantically as characters on *ER* and other hospital programs on television, but they have to be strong, alert, savvy people who can deal with any emergency.

When asked why they want to be nurses or teachers, people often say that it's because they love children. But teaching and nursing are two different ways of loving children and call for different types of people. Maybe not much attention was paid years ago to the differences between them because the jobs were lumped together as "women's work." Now that more men are going into both professions, however—even though the majority of nurses and elementary teachers are still women—the public is beginning to realize that these distinct careers demand two different sets of skills and character traits. For those considering them, the question is not which is better, but which is better for you?

1. Which plan of organization did Andrea use?
2. Is this essay primarily a comparison of similarities, of differences, or both?
3. What is the thesis, or main point, of Andrea's comparison? Which sentence could be considered a thesis statement?
4. How are the introductory and concluding paragraphs linked?
5. Identify the topic of each body paragraph.

6. What factual information helps you understand the point of Andrea's comparison?

7. What kind of additional information would strengthen the essay and help Andrea make her career decision?

Example by a Published Author: Comparing and Contrasting

Read the passage below, in which Howard Gardner compares and contrasts two famous psychologists, Sigmund Freud and William James, one European and the other American. Answer the questions afterward.

Two Great Psychologists
Howard Gardner

Freud and James represented different historical movements, different philosophical traditions, different programs for psychology. Freud, the pessimistic European intellectual, had chosen to focus on the development of the individual psyche, its battles within the individual's immediate family, the struggle for independence, the manifold anxieties and defenses that attend the human condition. For Freud the key to health was self-knowledge and a willingness to confront the inevitable pains and paradoxes of human existence.

James had considerable sympathy with this analysis, for his own life had featured many of the strains and tensions that Freud graphically described. Yet James also sensed a difference in the emphasis in their respective world views. While praising Freud, he had also pointed out to a confidant, "I hope that Freud and his pupils will push their ideas to the utmost limits, so that we can learn what they are.... It reveals an entirely unsuspected peculiarity in the constitution of human nature." James, in fact, had chosen to embrace a more positively oriented form of psychology, one less circumscribed by the biological imperatives of behavior, more open to the possibilities of change and growth. More so than his Austrian counterpart, the American thinker stressed the importance of relationships with other individuals, as a means of gaining ends, of effecting progress, and of knowing oneself. In a famous phrase, he had commented, "A man has as many social selves as there are individuals who recognize him and carry an image around of him in their mind." Perhaps most important, James was a potent influence on the succeeding generation of social scientists, including James Mark Baldwin and George Herbert Mead, who came to focus on the social origins of knowledge and on the interpersonal nature of an individual's sense of self.

But what united Freud and James, and what set them apart from the mainstream of psychology both on the Continent and in the United States, was a belief in the importance, the centrality, of the individual self—a conviction that psychology must be built around the concept of the person, his personality, his growth, his fate. Moreover, both scholars deemed the capacity for self-growth to be an important one, upon which depended the possibility of coping with one's surroundings. While neither would have used the phrase, I find it reasonable to say that both of these redoubtable psychologists were sympathetic to the idea of "personal intelligences." At the same time, however, their orientations toward such intelligences would have differed. Freud was interested in the self as located in the individual and, as a clinician, was preoccupied with an individual's own knowledge of himself; given this bias, a person's interest in other individuals was justified chiefly as a better means of gaining further understanding of one's own problems, wishes, and anxieties and, ultimately, of achieving one's goals. In contrast, James's interest, and even more so, the interests of the American social psychologists who succeeded him, fell much more on the individual's relationship to the outside community. Not only did one's knowledge of self come largely from an ever-increasing appreciation of how others thought about the individual; but the purpose of self-knowledge was less to promote one's personal agenda, more to ensure the smooth functioning of the community.

—Howard Gardner, from *Frames of Mind.*

1. Explain or look up the meaning of these words: *psyche, graphically, manifold, defenses, confidant, circumscribed, redoubtable, agenda.*

2. Which of the two psychologists does the author describe as more optimistic?

3. Which of the two was more interested in social relationships?

4. What similarities between Freud and James does the author describe?

5. What differences does he describe?

6. Describe the structure on which this comparison is based.

7. What, according to the author, made both psychologists different from others of their time?

WRITING TIP #10

When you first attempt to write a good comparison, you may feel lost and tangled up. Remember that feeling confused at the beginning may mean that you are doing the right thing: If your comparison is too neat and easy in the early stages, it probably means that you are still skimming the surface of the topic. To maintain your confidence, keep your eye on the main purpose of the comparison—gaining new insights into the two subjects you are comparing and into the overall concepts involved. If you compare two athletes or presidents, you hope not only to learn factual information about both but to gain a better understanding of how to evaluate an athlete's or a president's career. In comparing two short stories, you will probably notice details that you might otherwise have missed, and you will come away knowing more about how to analyze fiction.

Writing Exercises: Basic, Intermediate, Challenge

The following exercises provide practice in developing comparisons by using many supporting details.

☐ Basic Exercise: Comparison and Contrast

Rewrite the passage below, filling in details that show similarities and differences between living in a city and living in a small community. Write two or three sentences in each blank, supplying facts from your own experience or from what you have seen in films or television programs or learned from your reading or conversations with other people.

The physical surroundings in a small community are different from those of a city. A small town is quiet; you hear mostly

_____.

_____

_____.

A large city is noisy; you hear _____.

_____

_____.

A small town also looks different than a city. For instance, you see _____.

_____

_____.

In a metropolis, on the other hand, you are surrounded by ___

_____.

_____

_____.

The way people spend their time in a small community is also different from the pastimes city people engage in. In a small town, people mostly _____.

_____

_____.

Urban people, however, like to _____.

_____

_____.

However, there are some similarities between life in a small town and in a city. Certain kinds of shopping are almost the same in either place. For example, you can buy _____ anywhere. In addition, there are some things that people spend their time doing that are the same in both places. For instance, people in small towns and big cities all like to _____.

_____

_____ .

    With all their differences and similarities, I prefer to live in _____, because _____.

_____

_____ .

▨ Intermediate Exercise: Comparison and Contrast

In this brainstorming exercise, list as many facts as you can in each category that would help create body paragraphs for an interesting comparative essay.

Main Idea: Doing research in the library and doing research on the Internet require some different skills but have many similarities.

Different skills required:

Using the Internet:

1. _____

2. _____

3. _____

Using the library:

1. _____

2. _____

3. _____

Similarities:

1. _____

2. _____

3. _____

■ Challenge Exercise: Comparison and Contrast

This poem, written by Dudley Randall, is an imaginary conversation in verse between two famous African American leaders of the early twentieth century, Booker T. Washington and W. E. B. DuBois. They have different points of view on how to deal with racism in their time. Read the poem and answer the questions that follow.

Booker T. and W.E.B.

"It seems to me," said Booker T.,
"It shows a mighty lot of cheek
To study chemistry and Greek
When Mister Charlie needs a hand
To hoe the cotton on his land,
And when Miss Ann looks for a cook,
Why stick your nose inside a book?"
"I don't agree," said W.E.B.,
"If I should have the drive to seek
Knowledge of chemistry or Greek,
I'll do it. Charles and Miss can look
Another place for hand or cook.
Some men rejoice in skill of hand
And some in cultivating land,
But there are others who maintain
The right to cultivate the brain."
"It seems to me," said Booker T.,
"That all you folks have missed the boat
Who shout about the right to vote,
And spend vain days and sleepless nights
In uproar over civil rights.
Just keep your mouths shut, do not grouse,
But work, and save, and buy house."
"I don't agree," said W.E.B.,
"For what can property avail
If dignity and justice fail?
Unless you help to make the laws,
They'll steal your house with trumped-up clause.
A rope's as tight, a fire as hot,
No matter how much cash you've got.

Speak soft, and try your little plan,
But as for me, I'll be a man."
"It seems to me," said Booker T.—
"I don't agree,"
Said W.E.B.

1. This poem employs the point-by-point method of comparison. What are the two main topics about which the two leaders disagree in this poem?

2. How does each leader want his followers to behave?

3. What does each man assume about racism in American society?

4. These men were leaders of civil rights movements during the Reconstruction Period not long after the Civil War, when people remembered the days of slavery. Do a Web search on both men and read summaries of their careers. How can their argument be applied to our society today?

5. What differences can you detect between the two men's personalities?

6. Does the poem show a preference for one speaker or the other?

7. You probably side with one speaker or the other. How do the other speaker's points help you understand the problem of racism more clearly?

Essay Topics: Comparison/Contrast

1. Compare your attitudes toward marriage and family with those of your parents.

2. Compare your high school and college courses.

3. Compare two employers you have worked for.

4. Compare two television programs you watch frequently.

5. Compare two musical groups or athletic teams.

6. Compare attitudes toward family in the U.S. and in another country.

7. Compare two short stories or poems you have read.

PEER REVIEW QUESTIONS: COMPARISON/CONTRAST

1. I think that your overall purpose in comparing these two subjects is to make the following point:

2. Your introduction is interesting.   ☐ yes   ☐ no
Your introduction identifies the two subjects you are comparing.   ☐ yes   ☐ no
Your introduction and conclusion clearly express the thesis you are supporting in your comparison.   ☐ yes ☐ no

3. You analyze the following similarities between the two subjects:

4. You analyze the following differences between the two subjects:

5. You use the following method of organizing your comparison:

6. What I like best about your essay is the following:

7. I recommend that you make the following changes:

Proofreading Practice: Modifiers in Comparisons

Adjectives in Comparisons

Besides their simple forms, adjectives have two forms that are used in comparisons. The comparative form is used to compare two unequal things, and the superlative form is used to set one thing off from all the others.

Simple Form	Comparative Form	Superlative Form
good	better	best
young	younger	youngest
strong	stronger	strongest
easy	easier	easiest
happy	happier	happiest

Adjectives with three or more syllables always take **more** and **most** rather than the **–er** and **–est** endings.

beautiful	more beautiful	most beautiful
exciting	more exciting	most exciting

Your dictionary will show that some two-syllable words take *–er* and *–est*, while others take *more* and *most*.

heavy	heavier	heaviest
friendly	friendlier	friendliest
subtle	subtler	subtlest
cheerful	more cheerful	most cheerful
precise	more precise	most precise

Use the comparative form when comparing two things or people:

She is <u>wealthier</u> than her sister.

She is the <u>wealthier</u> of the two sisters.

(Remember to use *than*, not *then*, in making comparisons.)

Use the superlative form to set off one from a whole group:

She is the <u>wealthiest</u> woman in the group.

She is the <u>wealthiest</u> of the three sisters.

Adverbs in Comparisons

Adverbs also have comparative and superlative forms. Nearly all adverbs take *more* and *most*. The only exceptions are the few that serve as both adjectives and adverbs—*early, late, hard, fast, low*, and *straight*. These take *–er* and *–est*: *earlier, earliest*.

Simple Form	Comparative Form	Superlative Form
easily	more easily	most easily
violently	more violently	most violently
recently	more recently	most recently
happily	more happily	most happily

We also make negative comparisons, using adjectives and adverbs in combination with *less* or *least*.

expensive	less expensive	least expensive
difficult	less difficult	least difficult
safely	less safely	least safely
forcefully	less forcefully	least forcefully

Do not use *both* the *-er* or *-est* ending and the helping words *more*, *most*, *less*, or *least*.

Incorrect: You are <u>more better</u> than the last shortstop.

They are <u>less healthier</u> than they should be.

Correct: You are <u>better</u> than the last shortstop.

They are <u>less healthy</u> than they should be.

Incorrect: This was the <u>most saddest</u> film I have seen.

This was the <u>least richest</u> pastry on the menu.

Correct: This was the <u>saddest</u> film I have seen.

This was the <u>least rich</u> pastry on the menu.

TEST YOURSELF: ADJECTIVES AND ADVERBS IN COMPARISONS

Correct the errors in the passage below:

Harold has gained and lost weight many times. This has happened partly because he is an actor and some roles require him to be more heavier than others. He once had to play a protestor who went on a hunger strike, so he had to look much more skinnier than you usually does. He found it difficulter than he expected to lose thirty pounds for the role. Another time he played the role of a fat man and had to get much more bigger. To do this, he stuffed himself with pasta, pastries, and other foods with lots of fat and sugar. He had to do this more rapid than he wanted to because of a deadline. After he lost the extra weight he worked out until he was in the most fittest condition of his life. Then he got a role playing a soccer star and couldn't have been cast perfecter.

Answers: 1. to be heavier than others 2. look much skinnier 3. found it more difficult 4. to get much bigger 5. more rapidly than he wanted 6. in the fittest condition 7. more perfectly

Proofreading Exercises: Basic, Intermediate, Challenge

☐ **Basic Exercise: Adjectives and Adverbs in Comparisons**

Correct the seven errors in this passage.

Yolanda is very different from her sister. Yolanda is a more better student than Sonya, but Sonya is more sociable and popular. Although Yolanda is more young than Sonya, she has always been considered just as mature. Sonya, however, often takes the lead in social situations because she converses easier with others than her sister, especially with older people. In school Yolanda often helps her older sister with homework because she can read and memorize rapider than Sonya. They support each other in many ways and are the dependablest of friends in times of trouble. They also share all their secrets with each other, and no sisters could ever be more honester with each other then they are.

■ **Intermediate Exercise: Adjectives and Adverbs in Comparisons**

Correct the seven errors in this passage.

Attitudes of teenagers today toward dating and relationships are very different from those of their parents. Today's adolescents are less likelier to go on formal dates then their parents did. Instead they usually hang out with groups of friends and wait a longer time before getting married. They talk more easier about sex and gender roles than their parents did, and they are toleranter about questions of sexual preference. Their parents had more stronger beliefs about having children outside wedlock and were less readier to accept relationships between people of different religions and races. Today's teenagers are also used to women competing more confident with men than in the past.

■ **Challenge Exercise: Adjectives and Adverbs in Comparisons**

Correct the seven errors in this passage.

Experts debate whether medication or therapy is the effectiver way of treating depression. Before today's antidepressant drugs were discovered, all treatment had to be talk therapy, which sometimes produced recovery and sometimes did not. With the advent of Prozac and more recent developed drugs, claims were made that medications worked faster and with more greater effect. As combinations of therapy and medication achieved increasingly more higher levels of success with many patients, new studies were done to compare the methods of talk therapy and the use of medications. Although the results of such studies so far are less clearer than we might wish, some consensus is emerging that certain combinations of drugs and therapy are powerfuler modes of cure then either drugs or therapy alone.

CHAPTER 11
EXPLAINING A PROCESS OR PROCEDURE

Clarity and guiding your reader are the key principles to writing an essay about processes and procedures. When you explain how something happens or give instructions about how to do something, every step must be easy to follow. Achieving this means using clear language and a reader-friendly method of organizing your material. Imagine that you are the reader relying on your essay to provide you with complete information on a topic. Does your essay do that? Or, are there gaps where information is missing and passages where the meaning is ambiguous? Double meanings can enrich a poem, but they only confuse the reader of procedural writing. Use topic sentences at the beginning of every paragraph to signal each stage in the process or procedure you are describing. In explanatory writing, it is better to lean in the direction of being too mechanical and obvious than to risk being unclear.

"How-To" Writing: Giving Clear Instructions

If procedural writing is to succeed at guiding a reader through a process, it must be thorough. Procedural essays usually follow a step-by-step pattern of organization and leave nothing out. An instruction manual that tells you how to hook up a desktop computer, for instance, cannot contain confusing statements or omit anything you need to know; if it does, the computer will not work.

Most of us are used to giving instructions aloud and being able to rely on the aid of gestures, tone of voice, and listener feedback to help us navigate the process. As a writer, you cannot use these aids. You can get feedback while drafting your essay, but once you have completed your final version, your words alone have to say it all. The reader cannot ask you to explain what he or she does not understand.

A crucial step in ensuring that your reader understands what you are saying is making sure that she or he can understand your terminology. It is appropriate to use specialized terms when you are writing for experts on your topic, but if you are writing for general readers, use vocabulary only as technical as necessary and explain the meaning of all technical terms the first time you use them. Remember whom you are writing for: You will not write the same paragraph for general readers that you would for specialists.

Student Essay: Explaining a Procedure

Read the following student essay and answer the questions afterward.

How to Get the Most Out of a Course
Edgar Simms

Most of the students I know approach a course with the attitude, "How can I get an A in this course?" They need high grade point averages to be admitted to competitive programs and graduate schools, and all they care about is their grades. But they are missing out on another side of college education. They should ask themselves the question, "What can I get out of this course?" That includes a high grade, but there is much more to it. I have some advice on how to get the most out of any course you take.

First, figure out why you're taking the course and what you hope to learn from it. In some cases, you don't have a choice because the course is required. In a mandatory course, ask yourself what you really can learn that will be worthwhile to you, either as part of your major or as knowledge that will help you in your career. Then focus on that part of the course and relate everything else to it. For instance, if there's a term paper, do it on a topic that matters to you. And ask questions in class about your special interests. For instance, if you're taking a required economics course but you want to be a nurse or a doctor, ask questions about the economic problems in health care and write a term paper about medical malpractice.

When you choose elective courses, pick the ones that will really matter to you, not just courses taught by "hot" professors or ones that have a reputation for being easy. Sometimes a course that's too easy will bore you, and you end up not doing as well as you expected. If you take a more difficult course in astronomy, and you are really fascinated by what's being discovered about the possibility of life on other planets, you'll probably earn a good grade because you'll work hard without realizing it. Let your real interests guide you, and you'll do better.

There are also some pointers I can give about behavior that will help you do well in any class. Most students head for the back of the room and never say anything. They often make fun of students who sit at the front, wave their hands in the teacher's face, and do all the talking. Maybe you don't want to look like the "teacher's pet," but you should sit near the front and join all the class discussions. This isn't just to impress the teacher but to keep yourself interested in the course material and remember it better. When you talk a lot, and when other students disagree with you, you'll remember what went on much better than if you just sit at the back and pretend to take a few notes.

Another thing you should do, which you may avoid at first, is to go see your professors during their office hours. This isn't to earn a higher grade (although it may help sometimes) but to make the course part of your identity and remember what you learned in it. And, of course, if you're having trouble understanding anything in the course, it's even more important that you communicate with the professor and with a tutor, if one is available.

One last suggestion is to form a study group. Students in some cultures do this all the time, but most students in the U.S. aren't used to doing it. Try to find three or four other students in your class and meet once every week or two to discuss what's going on in the course. This will help you be interested in, understand, and remember the subject of the course.

All of these methods work. Use them. You'll get more out of every course you take. Remember that you're paying a lot of money for your education and putting a lot of time into it. Don't waste it. Besides, using these methods, chances are you'll earn a higher grade point average than the students who spend all their time trying to find easy courses, professors who give high grades, and methods of cheating on exams.

---

1. In your own words, identify the procedure Edgar explains in this essay.
2. How does he distinguish his approach from that of many other students?
3. In his opening paragraph, how does he seek to arouse interest in his subject?
4. How many parts does the body of his essay contain?
5. What are the two categories of courses he identifies?
6. What advice does he give for each separately? For all courses?
7. How clear are his points of advice? Could you follow them easily?

Analyzing a Process: Making the Connections

Organizing your material in a process essay can be easy. Follow a step-by-step plan or one that groups your explanation into a few categories, and do not wander from your main purpose. To make your explanation easy to follow, guide the reader by using transition words such as *before, next, then, afterward, however,* and *therefore* between paragraphs and occasionally between sentences within paragraphs. Help the reader to visualize the procedure by imagining yourself as the reader and mentally putting yourself through the process. Try to anticipate and prevent the reader's likely errors and misunderstandings by identifying and explaining the points where readers might take the wrong step or become confused. Include a few *FAQs*—frequently asked questions—to highlight the problem spots that most people run into as they become involved in whatever process you are explaining.

It is important to include sufficient information in procedural writing, but keep in mind one caution: avoid clutter. Do not editorialize or digress; include only information that will keep the reader on track. No matter how interesting irrelevant details may be, they distract readers by interrupting their trains of thought. When giving directions to a driver, for example, it is wise to avoid instructions such as, "When you pass the church, you'll see a turnoff on the right; don't take that." It is easier to say, "Take the second right."

Researching the Facts of the Process

To write a successful essay explaining a process or procedure, you must have correct information. A simple procedural essay based on personal experience will not require much research, but one involving technical details, sociological ideas, or scientific facts requires you to do some reading. Obviously, an essay explaining how the Federal Reserve System affects the economy requires specialized knowledge, as does an essay explaining how to acquire a patent on a new invention. Students usually write essays about subjects they are familiar with, but even when you feel confident about your grasp of a process, do some preliminary reading and research to make sure that you have enough facts and that your facts are correct. And when you use other sources of information, you *must* cite them properly. (Procedures for quoting, paraphrasing, and preparing a bibliography are explained in Chapter 14.)

Example by Published Author: Explaining a Process

Process analysis gives a step-by-step account of how something develops. It is similar to procedural writing, but instead of giving someone instructions, in process analysis you are describing a social phenomenon or an institutional structure. For example, read the following explanation by Jane Jacobs from her well-known book on American cities, *The Death and Life of Great American Cities*, and answer the questions that follow.

The Kind of Problem a City Is

Jane Jacobs

Big cities and countrysides can get along well together. Big cities need countryside close by. And countryside—from man's point of view—needs big cities, with all their diverse opportunities and productivity, so human beings can be in a position to appreciate the rest of the natural world instead of to curse it.

Being human is itself difficult, and therefore all kinds of settlements (except dream cities) have problems. Big cities have difficulties in abundance. But vital cities are not helpless to combat even the most difficult of problems. They are not passive victims of chains of circumstances, any more than they are the malignant opposite of nature.

Vital cities have marvelous innate abilities for understanding, communicating, contriving and inventing what is required to combat their difficulties. Perhaps the most striking example of this ability is the effect that big cities have had on disease. Cities were once the most helpless and devastated victims of disease, but they became great disease conquerors. All the apparatus of surgery, hygiene, microbiology, chemistry, telecommunications, public health measures, teaching and research hospitals, ambulances and the like, which people not only in cities but also outside them depend upon for the unending war against premature mortality, are fundamentally products of big cities and would be inconceivable without big cities. The surplus wealth, the productivity, the close-grained juxtaposition of talents that permit society to support advances such as these are themselves products of our organization into cities, and especially into big and dense cities.

It may be romantic to search for the salves of society's ills in slow-moving rustic surroundings, or among innocent, unspoiled provincials, if such exist, but it is a waste of time. Does anyone suppose that, in real life, answers to any of the great questions that worry us today are going to come out of homogeneous settlements?

Dull, inert cities, it is true, do contain the seeds of their own destruction and little else. But lively, diverse, intense cities contain the seeds of their own regeneration, with energy enough to carry over for problems and needs outside themselves.

—Jane Jacobs, from *The Death and Life of Great American Cities*.

1. Explain or look up the meaning of these words and phrases: *malignant, innate, premature mortality, juxtaposition, provincials, homogeneous settlements, inert.*

2. How does Jane Jacobs explain the ability of cities to overcome problems?

3. What specific problem does she mention that cities overcame?

4. How does she describe the relationship between the cities and the countryside?

5. What kind of cities does she believe have the power to overcome serious problems?

6. What quality do cities have that tend toward self-destruction?

7. What kinds of communities are not likely to provide solutions to the big social problems?

WRITING TIP #11

Make sure your procedural essay is clear by reading it aloud to a number of people separately. Ask your listeners whether anything confuses them, and do not be satisfied until they consistently understand everything you say. If you are writing a memo, try it out on coworkers and have them explain your instructions in their own words. It is harder than you might expect to write instructions that every reader can understand and follow correctly. We live in a visual culture; people want to see procedures and processes and become impatient with written instructions. So, make yours crisp and reader-friendly.

Writing Exercises: Basic, Intermediate, Challenge

☐ Basic Exercise: Procedural Writing

Below is a plan for an essay explaining how to prepare for and execute a successful job interview. Answer the questions that follow.

Essay Plan

Introduction: What Makes an Effective Interview
I. Planning
II. Creating a Favorable First Impression
III. Successful Strategies for the Interview
IV. Some Things to Avoid
V. Following Up
Conclusion: Final Thoughts

1. What do you think are the most important elements of interviewing to stress in your introduction?
2. What kind of planning do you think will strengthen an interview?
3. In Section II, how can a prospective employee enhance his or her first impression?
4. In Section III, name some of the most important strategies to remember in the interview itself.
5. In Section IV, what do you think are the two or three things to avoid that could ruin a good interview?
6. In Section V, what do you recommend that a prospective employee should do to follow up after an interview?
7. In your conclusion, what overall attitude toward effective interviewing do you want the reader to gain from your essay?

Intermediate Exercise: Procedural Writing

Read the following explanation from Dr. Spock's famous book, *Baby and Child Care*, and answer the questions that follow.

Helping Children with Their Lessons
Benjamin Spock, M.D., and Steven J. Parker, M.D.

Sometimes a teacher will advise parents that their child is falling behind and needs tutoring in a subject. Sometimes the parents have the idea themselves. This is something to be careful about. If the school can recommend a good tutor whom you can afford, go ahead and hire him. Too often parents make poor tutors, not because they don't know enough, not because they don't try hard enough, but because they care too much and become too upset when their child doesn't understand. I learned that as a seven-year-old. If a child is already mixed up in his lessons, an impatient parent may be the last straw. Another trouble is that the parents' method may be different from that being used in class. If the child is already baffled by the subject as presented in school, the chances are that he will be even more baffled when it's presented in a different way at home.

I don't want to go so far as to say that a parent should never tutor a child, because in some cases it works very well. I'd only advise a parent to talk it over thoroughly with the teacher first, and then quit right away if it isn't going well. Whoever is tutoring the child should keep in touch with the teacher, at regular intervals.

What should you do if children ask for help with their homework? If they are puzzled and turn to you for clarification, there's no harm in straightening them out. (Nothing pleases parents more than to have a chance occasionally to prove to a child that they really know something.) But if your children are asking you to do their work for them because they don't understand it, you'd better consult the teacher. A good teacher prefers to help children understand and then let them rely on themselves. If the teacher is too busy to give your child some extra time, you may have to lend a hand; but even then you should just help him to understand his work; you should not do it for him. Your child can have many teachers but only one mother and father. Your role as parent is more important.

Relations between Parent and Teacher

It's easy to get along with the teacher if your son is the teacher's pride and joy and doing well in class. But if your child is having trouble, the situation is more delicate. The best parents and the best teachers are all very human. All take pride in the work they are doing and have possessive feelings toward the child. Each, no matter how reasonable, secretly feels that the child would be doing better if the other would only handle him a little differently. It's helpful to the parents to realize at the start that the teacher is just as sensitive as they are, and that they will get further in a conference by being friendly and cooperative.

Some parents are afraid of facing a teacher, but they forget that just as often the teacher is afraid of them. The parents' main job is to give a clear history of the child's past, what his interests are, and what he responds to well or badly and then to work with the teacher on how best to apply this information in school. Don't forget to compliment the teacher on those parts of the class program that are a great success with the child.

Occasionally a child and teacher just don't "fit" temperamentally, no matter how hard they both work at it. In these cases, the principal can be involved in the question of whether to move the child to another class.

Parents should avoid blaming the teacher if their child is unsuccessful in class. If the child hears the parents bad-mouthing the teacher, he will learn to blame others and to avoid taking responsibility for his contribution to his problems. You can still be sympathetic: "I know how hard you are trying," or "I know how unhappy it makes you when your teacher is dissatisfied."

—Benjamin Spock, M.D., and Steven J. Parker, M.D.,
from *Dr. Spock's Baby and Child Care.*

1. Identify the categories Dr. Spock uses to organize the material in this passage.

2. What's the first thing he says parents should do if their child has trouble in school?

3. What are two reasons parents sometimes do not make good tutors?

4. What does Dr. Spock recommend if your child asks for help with homework?

5. What does he caution against doing when a child asks for help?

6. What attitude does he say parents and teachers often have toward one another?

7. What, according to Dr. Spock, is the difference between the roles of parents and teachers?

■ Challenge Exercise: Procedural Writing

Choose a procedure you know how to do, such as parking a car, buying a dress, ordering a product online, preparing and giving a speech, planning a wedding, planning a trip, or doing a workout at the gym. Write answers to the following questions:

1. Identify at least four or five steps or categories you could use in writing an explanation about this procedure.
   List these steps or categories in the most effective order.

2. Identify at least two problem spots—phases of the procedure where things might go wrong or the reader might make a mistake.
   Explain why it is important to avoid these errors.

3. Identify one example where your personal experience might help to enliven your explanation.

4. Name several transitional words and phrases you would use in moving from one section of your explanation to the next.

5. Identify the underlying assumptions you make about your subject that you would want your reader to share.

Essay Topics: Procedural Writing

Choose one of the following topics and write a "how-to" or procedural essay. Begin with a concise, clear statement of purpose and develop your discussion step by step, using transitional words. Be sure to obtain and fact-check the necessary information, either by doing Internet research or by reading articles or books on the subject.

1. How to shop on the Internet
2. How to eat what you like but stay thin
3. How to prepare for a career in _____
4. How a baby develops in the first year
5. How popular music has changed in the last decade
6. How the demographics of your state have changed in the last decade
7. How advice on nutrition has changed since the 1990s

PEER REVIEW QUESTIONS: PROCEDURAL AND PROCESS WRITING

1. Here is my impression of what you are explaining in your essay:

2. Your introduction is interesting. ☐ yes ☐ no
   Your introduction makes the purpose of your essay clear. ☐ yes ☐ no
   The sentence that most nearly expresses your main point is the following:

3. You explain the process or procedure in a clear, step-by-step sequence. ☐ yes ☐ no

4. Your explanation is thorough and leaves nothing out. ☐ yes ☐ no

5. Your conclusion (is/is not) effective for the following reason:

6. What I like best about your essay is the following:

7. I recommend you make the following changes:

Proofreading Practice: Present and Progressive Tenses

Writing about a process or procedure mostly involves the present tense: You are explaining how something occurs in general rather than describing a single event that happened in the past. Using the present tense, of course, requires you to watch your *s*-endings carefully: use the *s*-ending for singular (she <u>writes</u>); do not use the ending for plural (they <u>write</u>).For non-native speakers of English, the present tense is often hard to distinguish from the **progressive tense**, which is the form created by adding *–ing* to the verb in combination with a form of *be* (am, is, are).

What is the difference between the two phrases below?

Susan <u>writes</u>.

Susan <u>is writing</u>.

Both are in the present tense, but the second is called the **present progressive**. This form refers to an action caught in the moment when it is happening, whereas the **simple present** refers to general actions that take place repeatedly. For instance, we can say,

Susan <u>writes</u> to her sister every week.

Susan <u>is writing</u> at this very moment.

When explaining a process, you will use mostly the **simple present**, but you might need the **present progressive** to tell about one procedure while something else is happening. For example, "Don't disconnect the set while the battery <u>is charging</u>" or "While you <u>are compiling</u> the guest list, don't forget to include the groom's friends."

TEST YOURSELF: PRESENT AND PRESENT PROGRESSIVE TENSES

Correct the errors in the verb forms below. One sentence is correct.

1. Alice always go to the supermarket on Fridays.
2. Some of the money is belonging to Fred's uncle.
3. This difficult step in the procedure require preparation.
4. The instruction manual is explaining how to install the program.
5. Prolonged wars usually causes inflation.
6. A bridge is being constructed over the bay.
7. The cookbook suggest preheating the oven for 10 minutes.

Answers: 1. goes 2. belongs 3. requires 4. explains 5. cause 6. correct 7. suggests

Proofreading Exercises: Basic, Intermediate, Challenge

☐ Basic Exercise: Present and Present Progressive Tenses

Correct the verb errors in the sentences below. One sentence is correct.

1. Every Saturday Jeremy attend a biology class.

2. Carla should be the parliamentarian because she is knowing *Robert's Rules of Order.*

3. Stage acting demand both physical and emotional effort.

4. John liked the film because it is ending with a hilarious twist.

5. Global warming cause the polar ice cap to melt.

6. The population of the Southwest is increasing.

7. Opening the package require a pair of scissors.

■ Intermediate Exercise: Present and Present Progressive Tenses

Correct the seven errors in this passage:

In December 2004, people around the world became familiar with the word *tsunami.* Based on Japanese words for wave and harbor, *tsunami* is referring to a huge tidal wave created by an earthquake. When an earthquake occur underneath the sea, as it did near Sumatra in Southeast Asia, it creates a wall of water that move through the ocean at tremendous speeds. When it reaches a seashore, it is slowing down but still may travel at one hundred miles an hour. First it produces a huge undertow that can suck all the water back from the shoreline. Then it is hitting the beach in a series of waves that can be 20, 30, even 100 feet high. People often do not see a tsunami coming in time to evacuate the coast. Unlike hurricanes, which meteorologists can forecast days in advance, tidal waves is harder to predict. As a result, devastating loss of life often is resulting, as in Indonesia, Sri Lanka, India, and Thailand in December 2004.

■ Challenge Exercise: Present and Present Progressive Tenses

Correct the seven errors in this passage:

The first telescopes used to study the stars and planets were refracting telescopes, which uses two main lenses to magnify images. An important step in astronomy occurred when Sir Isaac Newton built the first reflecting telescope, which use two mirrors instead of lenses. Mirrors improve magnification and light gathering power in several ways. First, mirrors can be made larger than the largest lenses and thus gathers more light. In addition, mirrors do not have the problem of bending different colors of light at different angles as lenses are doing, and thus can focus images more sharply. A reflecting telescope has a large mirror at the back, which gathers the incoming light and is focusing it through a smaller mirror at the front, which reflects it through a magnifying eyepiece. The light is traveling twice the length of the tube, thus allowing for twice as much magnification as a refracting telescope of the same length. The large telescopes built in the twentieth century, such as the Hale Telescope on Mt. Palomar in California, are modeled on a reflecting design, but are containing many modern improvements over Isaac Newton's simple instrument.

CHAPTER 12
ANALYZING CAUSE AND EFFECT

Analyzing causes and effects can be simple or complicated and intellectually profound. At any level of difficulty, your intention when examining cause and effect is to reveal something to readers that they might not see—for example, the causes of teenage rebellion or high dropout rates, the benefits of exercise, or the effects of video games on children. College assignments often involve analysis of cause and effect because exploring either **why something happens** or **what results from something** exercises your brain in many ways at once. You have to think logically, remain open to complexities, search out the facts, and organize your material clearly. **Analyzing causes** requires you to think backward from a point in time and explain what caused a known situation. **Analyzing effects** means thinking ahead from a point in time, looking at a known situation and explaining what resulted or will result from that situation. The two examples below explore these topics: The student essay looks at a well-known fact—the existence of community colleges—and figures out why there are so many of them. The reading by a published author (a noted historian) begins with a well-known fact—the lack of jobs during the Great Depression of the 1930s—and analyzes what happened to people who lost their jobs. Both writers analyze cause and effect but in opposite directions.

Student Essay: Analyzing Causes

Where Community Colleges Came From
Michael Capella

A hundred years ago in the United States, there were elementary schools, high schools, and colleges, but no community colleges. Only in the last half of the twentieth century were community colleges beginning to appear in most states across the country. Now there are so many that a large percentage of college students, probably about one-third, attend community colleges. Why, we may ask, did this new kind of institution spring up, and why did it catch on? There are three main reasons.

One reason why community colleges are popular and necessary is that there are so many nontraditional students. These are students who are different from the students of the past who came from well-off families, lived in dormitories or sorority or fraternity houses, spent time going to football games and parties, and graduated in four years at the age of 21 or 22. Nontraditional students may be older, have families to support, hold down jobs, take courses part-time, commute to campus, and speak first languages other than English. They may come from other countries, and their parents may not speak English at all. Also, they may not come to college with a good knowledge of math and science, either because they studied them years ago in high school, or because they dropped out of high school and earned a G.E.D.

These nontraditional students usually can't afford to attend traditional four-year colleges, even if they are admitted to them. They fit in much better at community colleges, where they can take longer to graduate by going part-time and may be able to take remedial courses in subjects in which they are weak. The older students, such as women who didn't have a chance to go to college after high school and want a college degree after they have raised their children, may feel out of place on campuses full of 18-year-olds.

Another reason why community colleges are appearing everywhere is that they often have courses and degree programs connected to nearby job opportunities. In states with many insurance companies, they may offer special courses that train students to work in the insurance field. In communities with many job opportunities in banking or hotel management, they may offer career training in those areas. Since many of the students at community colleges need well-paying jobs that won't take them many years to obtain, they often choose career training like nursing, computer science, and finance.

The most important reason why community colleges are so numerous is that the job market has changed. Jobs that used to require a high school diploma now demand at least an associate's degree. Years ago, every student had the opportunity to get a free high school education; nowadays, every student who graduates from high school in most states has a chance to get a community college education that is not very expensive. More skills and knowledge are required for almost any decent-paying job than in the past, so community colleges are necessary to give everyone a chance. And many students who aren't sure whether they can make it in college turn out to be top students and go on to earn higher degrees. Some even become teachers, doctors, and lawyers.

Anybody who has gone to a community college can see why community colleges were necessary to fill a big gap in American education. If only teenage students from well-to-do families who earned top grades in high school were allowed to attend college, most of today's undergraduates would be out of luck. Community colleges came along to give everybody a chance to pursue their dreams—and they still do that.

1. Identify the thesis of this essay and the thesis statement.

2. How many causes does Michael name for the proliferation of community colleges?

3. Identify each cause. Which one seems most important to Michael? Where does he put it in the essay, and why?

4. Explain the difference between a traditional and nontraditional student.

5. What details does Michael bring in to describe traditional and nontraditional students?

6. How does he support his point that community colleges help students get jobs?

7. Name one or two additional reasons why community colleges have become important.

Example by a Published Author: Analyzing Effects

The following passage describes the effects of the Great Depression of the 1930s on unemployed people around the world. Read the selection and answer the questions afterward.

The Effect of Unemployment during the Great Depression

John A. Garraty

Many of the unemployed suffered from a lack of proper clothing and from poor housing. Social workers often reported that children of their clients could not go to school because they had no shoes. Many families suffered cruelly in winter because they had no money for coal or wood. It is true that landlords frequently allowed destitute families to remain in their flats out of pity or, the chance of finding another tenant being small, because they preferred having the places occupied in order to prevent them from being vandalized. But the press was full of stories of people evicted for nonpayment of rent or forced to part with their homes because they could not meet mortgage payments.

There was a big increase in vagrancy as people lost their homes and as the jobless took to the road in search of work. Lodging houses operated by local governments and by charitable organizations such as the Salvation Army took care of many of these unfortunates. On the borders of cities from Adelaide and Sydney in Australia to Buenos Aires in Argentina, shantytowns sprang up as groups of homeless people constructed ramshackle shelters on vacant land. One of the most elaborate of these places was the Village of Misery on the northwest outskirts of Vienna, with its shacks made of broken bricks, rusting stovepipes, and other discarded building materials.

The Australians gave these settlements names ranging from Hungry Mile to the sardonic Happy Valley; they called the shacks, constructed of packing cases, scrap lumber, and sheets of rusting metal, "humpies." At first Americans gave their shantytowns similar names—Hardluck-on-the-River, for example, and Prosperity

Park. But soon they began to call them Hoovervilles, an indication of what the result of the 1932 election was likely to be. In France the shantytowns received a more politically neutral name, *bidonvilles*, or tin can cities.

—John A. Garraty, excerpts from *The Great Depression.*

1. What do these words mean: *destitute, vandalized, evicted, mortgage, sardonic*?

2. How did the era's unemployment affect families?

3. Why did some landlords not evict people who couldn't pay rent?

4. What did some people do who had no homes?

5. Which countries are mentioned in this passage?

6. Why did some homeless people in America name their shanty-towns Hoovervilles?

7. In your opinion, does unemployment have a similar effect on people today?

Being Logical: Causes vs. Coincidences

The Latin phrase *post hoc ergo propter hoc* translates to *after something, therefore because of something.* This familiar mistake in logic simply means that you cannot assume one event causes another simply because the second event comes after the first. For instance, if I wore a yellow tie in the morning and it rained in the afternoon, and I believed the yellow tie had caused the rain, I would be guilty of making this mistake. Most of us engage in this kind of superstitious thinking once in a while, but we should avoid it when writing a cause and effect analysis.

How can you tell whether something really is a cause or effect, and not just a coincidence? Consider these examples; which would you say are logically connected?

• Poverty and terrorism
• Video games and students' performance in school
• Cell phones and automobile accidents

- Signs of the zodiac and world events
- Immigration and unemployment
- Players' salaries and winning teams
- The number 13 and bad luck
- Hollywood films and teenage behavior

Several of these pairs can be shown by evidence to be connected. Which ones cannot? What seems obvious and logical to one person may not seem that way to someone else. However, when you write an essay analyzing causes or effects, it is your job to explain connections convincingly. It is not enough to claim, for example, that the crime rate in a particular city dropped when a particular mayor was in office and therefore he or she necessarily caused the drop. What additional information would you need to decide whether the mayor helped reduce the rate of crime? What if other cities whose mayors used different methods of policing experienced equal drops in crime? How can we determine what causes crime to go up or down?

Identifying All the Causes and Effects

Whether discussing the crime rate, education, or a personal situation, you are usually better off assuming that there is more than one cause or effect for any given situation. Keep your mind open to all the possibilities. If most problems were so simple that one obvious cause or effect could be identified easily, sociologists, economists, psychologists, and historians would not be busy writing books arguing about causes and effects of such subjects as the causes of the two World Wars and the Great Depression, the results of global warming, and the future of the economy. Obviously, these are complex and controversial questions.

Finding the Necessary Information

To write a convincing analysis of cause and effect, you need factual information. Even in essays that are not primarily research papers, you should strengthen your analysis with factual information whenever you can. Rather than simply giving your opinion on whether capital punishment does or does not reduce the murder rate, do a Web search and look up an article or two that will provide statistics on the subject. If you are explaining why so many high school students drop out of school, gather information on dropout rates and what the experts have said on the subject. If you limit your analysis to your own school and your own observations, you still can write a valuable essay, but it will not clarify the larger problem as well as an essay in which you begin with your own observations but move on to analyze the problem using reliable data.

> ## WRITING TIP #12
>
> Cause and effect analysis is one of the most interesting modes of composition. It holds some dangers for the writer, however: it can be easy to lose your objectivity and become obsessed with a single cause or effect. Many factors are at play in most situations and for most topics, personal or social. Try to examine the problem with patience and openness. Of course your essay will express your strong point of view, but avoid arriving at your conclusions before you have considered the whole range of possible causes or effects. In addition, do some thoughtful prewriting. This extra intellectual effort will make your essay stronger and more convincing.

Writing Exercises: Basic, Intermediate, Challenge

☐ Basic Exercise: Cause and Effect

Practice identifying several causes and effects for every topic. For each of the topics below, list at least three causes or effects. Underline the one that you believe to be most important.

1. Name three reasons why you are attending college.

2. Name three reasons why your neighborhood has gotten better or worse.

3. Name three reasons why the enrollment in your college has gone up or down.

4. Name three causes of happiness in your life.

5. Name three ways technology has changed your life.

6. Name three ways having a baby has affected the life of someone you know.

7. Name three ways your college degree will improve your life.

▣ Intermediate Exercise: Cause and Effect

Practice identifying several causes and effects for every topic. Brainstorm each of the topics below and list at least three causes or effects. Underline the one that you believe to be most important.

1. Name three causes of high dropout rates in public schools.

2. Name three reasons why young people marry later today.

3. Name three reasons why students take online courses.

4. Name three reasons why immigrants come to the United States.

5. Name three effects of divorce on children.

6. Name three effects of sports teams on college campuses.

7. Name three effects of computer technology on jobs.

▣ Challenge Exercise: Cause and Effect

Analyze the cause-and-effect statements below and identify mistakes in logical reasoning. Improve each statement so that it contains a more logical connection between cause and effect.

1. The scientists who tell us about global warming must be right. It was much warmer this month in my home state than it was a year ago.

2. Men must be smarter at science than women because there are three times as many men as there are women earning Ph.D.s in physics in the United States.

3. If children continue to spend time playing video games, the rate of violence in schools will certainly increase rapidly.

4. The sources of Jason's information must be reliable because he found all of them in the library rather than on the Internet.

5. All of today's Olympic athletes must be using steroids because they keep breaking the records of earlier athletes.

6. People who live in the suburbs are happier than people who live in small towns because suburbanites earn larger incomes.

7. If all countries spoke the same language there would be no wars because wars are always between nations that speak different languages.

Essay Topics: Cause and Effect

Write an essay on one of the following topics. Do some preliminary thinking and prewriting activities. Base your analysis on both your own observation and information you can find about the topic on the Internet.

1. Explain what is causing the problem of obesity in America.

2. Explain why reality television shows are popular.

3. Explain why many young people do not vote in the United States.

4. Explain what causes eating disorders in many young women and men.

5. Analyze how cell phones and e-mail affect the behavior of young people.

6. Analyze how speaking English as a second language affects a student's college experience.

7. Analyze how blogs (Web logs) are influencing journalism and politics.

PEER REVIEW QUESTIONS: CAUSE AND EFFECT

1. My impression of your essay is that you are explaining the <u>cause</u> or <u>effect</u> (circle which) of _____ .

2. Your introduction is interesting. ☐ yes ☐ no
   Your introduction makes the purpose of your essay clear. ☐ yes ☐ no
   The sentence that most nearly expresses your main point is the following:

3. You identify the following causes (or effects):

4. Your analysis is logical and not oversimplified. ☐ yes ☐ no

5. Your conclusion (is/is not) effective for the following reason:

6. What I like best about your essay is the following:

7. I recommend you make the following changes:

Proofreading Practice: Compound and Complex Sentences

When you write a cause and effect analysis, you will often use transition words such as *if, so, whenever, because, therefore, as a result,* and *consequently* to connect the parts of your analysis. Using these transitions, however, requires a mastery of certain kinds of compound and complex sentences. Remember that sentences beginning with *if, whenever, when,* and *because* are **complex sentences**. That means that the first part is a **dependent clause** that should be followed by a comma.
Examples:

<u>If</u> it rains on Wednesday, we will have the party inside.

<u>Because</u> the customers prefer ATMs, the bank reduced the number of tellers.

However, sentences connected by *therefore, as a result, as a consequence, consequently,* and *hence* are **compound sentences** that require semicolons. The short connective word *so,* on the other hand, is preceded by a comma.
Examples:

The first paychecks were late; as a result, many workers were angry.

The college changed its financial aid policy; therefore, many students were unable to attend.

The combination of music and cinematography was perfect, so the film won many awards.

TEST YOURSELF: COMPOUND AND COMPLEX SENTENCES

Be careful to distinguish between compound sentences that require semicolons and complex sentences that require commas. Identify the correct sentences in the following group and correct the wrong ones.

1. The second floor is closed this week, consequently, we will hold the meeting in a classroom on the third floor.

2. Because the music was not difficult to read; Ted was able to recognize the melody.

3. Stricter immigration laws were passed, so it became harder to get a visa.

4. Sales figures dropped during March; therefore, analysts expected a decline in stock prices.

5. Whenever medication is combined with therapy. Patients with this condition tend to improve quickly.

6. Short stories usually focus on brief periods of time, as a result, the reader cannot see characters develop as they do in novels.

7. If you follow these instructions and use the map, your trip should take only three hours.

Answers: 1. ; consequently 2. read, 3. correct 4. correct 5. therapy, patients 6. time; 7. correct

Proofreading Exercises: Basic, Intermediate, Challenge

☐ Basic Exercise: Compound and Complex Sentences

Three of the sentences below are correct; identify them and correct the other four.

1. Whenever Jennifer has a cold. She takes echinacea and vitamin C.
2. Samuel prepared well for the test, so he felt confident.
3. Species adapt differently to changes in climate, therefore some thrive better than others.
4. Too many accidents occurred at the intersection consequently the city installed a traffic light.
5. Because illegal immigrants often work for low wages. Some employers prefer to hire them.
6. The book was difficult to read; hence many students left the assignment incomplete.
7. If the city pays part of the cost, the stadium will probably be built.

■ Intermediate Exercise: Compound and Complex Sentences

Compose sentences on the following models. Be sure to use correct punctuation.

1. Because the company's network was down, the work schedule had to be revised.

   Your sentence:

   Because _____, _____.

2. Whenever the registration period begins, students hurry to sign up for the best courses.

   Your sentence:

   Whenever _____, _____.

3. If the bill passes in the state senate, the governor will probably veto it.

Your sentence:

If _____, _____.

4. A writing section was added to the test; consequently, the tutors changed their methods.

Your sentence:

_____; consequently, _____.

5. The first CD sold five million copies; as a result, the company put out a second one immediately.

Your sentence:

_____; as a result, _____.

6. Jobs in computer science declined sharply; therefore, fewer students chose that major.

Your sentence:

_____; therefore, _____.

7. Elsie grew up among farm animals, so she decided to become a veterinarian.

Your sentence:

_____, so _____.

■ Challenge Exercise: Compound and Complex Sentences

In the paragraph below, find and correct the seven errors in sentence structure.

Many arguments have been put forward to explain the drop in violent crimes in large cities. Because the decline has been steady over a number of years; experts assume there must be identifiable reasons for it. If improved police work has been one of the causes. City mayors should be aware of that fact. However, other causes have been considered, therefore, it is a good idea to recognize the complexities of the problem. The crack epidemic has abated somewhat hence the crimes resulting from it have declined. Furthermore, the population of young men in the cities—at least those not already incarcerated—has dipped steadily as well, this, too, has contributed to the reduction of crime. Some sociologists have also argued that there have been fewer unwanted pregnancies in recent years, particularly among teenage women, as a result, fewer children grow up to be dysfunctional adults. Among all these possible causes, experts cannot reach a consensus on the chief reason why crime has gone down, therefore, they are still doing studies about it.

CHAPTER 13
ARGUING PERSUASIVELY

Writing that explains why the reader should believe or do something is called **persuasive writing**. In this kind of writing you are trying to reinforce or change someone's opinion. Persuasive writing is everywhere: in political speeches and debates, in newspapers and broadcast news editorials, in lawyers' courtroom speeches, in sales promotions, and in books advocating change in domestic and foreign policies.

Nearly every attempt at persuasion is based on an idea that can be expressed in one thesis statement. The speaker or writer argues that something *should* or *ought* to be done. Persuasive writing frequently uses words such as *should, ought, might, must, have to, could, probably, likely, possibly, certainly,* and *undoubtedly*. Learn to use them correctly in your own essays. Such words measure what the writer thinks should be changed in people's attitudes or actions. These words signal *why* relationships—and they usually end with a call to action.

The essay below takes a position on capital punishment, a well-worn topic that has been debated for centuries and continues to provoke us through high profile criminal cases and changes in the laws. Read the essay and answer the questions afterward.

Student Essay

Why the Death Penalty Is a Bad Idea

Melissa O'Brian

In many states, the death penalty is still practiced, and many voters favor it. In most countries outside the United States, however, it has been ended. Countries that have the death penalty, in fact, cannot be members of the European Union, and Pope John Paul II spoke out against it. Why is it that so many people in this country still favor the death penalty, even though most of the world disagrees? I think it is because many criminals who commit horrible crimes deserve an extreme punishment, and people react emotionally to these crimes, ignoring the reasons why it is wrong for society to practice capital punishment. But the fact remains, the death penalty is wrong in principle as well as in practice.

We all know about crimes that are so cruel and vicious that we want the perpetrators to get what they deserve. And we also read about criminals such as predators of children who get out of jail and repeat their terrible crimes. To some people these examples prove that the death penalty is justified. I agree that it is hard to claim that such wrongdoers do not deserve to die, but the question is, should society try to give them what they deserve out of revenge? Law courts are not intended to take revenge on criminals but to carry out justice. In many cases, we know how awful the crime was, but we often can't be one hundred percent sure that the person convicted is the one who did it. Justice requires that a punishment that cannot be reversed such as the death penalty should never be given to someone when there is even a slight chance that the wrong person has been sentenced.

There have been many cases overturned by using DNA analysis, so we now know that it is possible to execute innocent people—and probably some states already have done so. Many prisoners on death row have been released who were already sentenced for crimes they did not commit. And what about criminals who may have committed the crimes but maybe acted out of self-defense, insanity, or other factors that might deserve some other penalty? And should we execute criminals who can serve society behind bars? When the former gang leader Tookie Williams was executed in California in 2005, many of his supporters believed he had set a good example by writing children's books that warned young people to stay out of gangs. How many people on death row might be in some of these categories? It is against the principles of a democratic society to execute people under these circumstances where there is any doubt about their crimes or when rehabilitation is possible.

In practice, the death penalty does not work very well. Some juries are biased against groups of people they do not like and apply the death penalty unfairly. It also costs too much to execute criminals. Some people imagine that all society has to do is catch murderers and rapists and execute them right away, but that is not what happens. It takes millions of dollars in court costs and legal fees to convict someone and put them on death row. And after that there are many appeals that can take years and cost much more. It may be true that it costs a lot of money to keep inmates in prison but not as much as the expense of death penalty trials.

One of the main arguments for capital punishment is that it is supposed to make other criminals think twice before they commit murder. But most studies show that there is not much of a connection between states that have the death penalty and a drop in violent crimes. People who commit murder usually do not expect to get caught, or they are so desperate or insane that they do not care whether they are caught. Many people who commit crimes of passion, for instance, kill themselves afterward; obviously the death penalty would not stop them from doing the crime.

People who favor the death penalty should realize that they are reacting out of emotion, not reason and common sense. They want to get back at someone who commits the worst of crimes. They may be right in their feelings, but in principle capital punishment is wrong and uncivilized, and in practice it costs society and taxpayers too much to be worth the emotional satisfaction some people get from it.

---

1. Identify the thesis statement in this essay.
2. Explain what Melissa is trying to do in her introductory paragraph.
3. Explain what similarities you see between the introductory and concluding paragraphs.

4. How many points does Melissa make against the death penalty? What are they?

5. What counter-arguments does she bring up? How does she answer them?

6. Which is her strongest argument? Which is her weakest?

7. How could she strengthen her arguments by doing research?

Example by a Published Author

Is Cloning Wrong?
Lee M. Silver

Some object to cloning because of the process that it entails. The view of the Vatican, in particular, is that human embryos should be treated like human beings and should not be tampered with in any way. However, the cloning protocol does *not* tamper with embryos, it tampers only with *unfertilized* eggs and adult cells like those we scratch off our arms without a second thought. Only after the fact does an embryo emerge (which could be treated with the utmost respect if one so chooses).

There is a sense among some who are religious that cloning leaves God out of the process of human creation, and that man is venturing into places he does not belong. This same concern has been, and will continue to be, raised as each new reprogenetic technology is incorporated into our culture, from in vitro fertilization twenty years ago to genetic engineering of embryos—sure to happen in the near future. It is impossible to counter this theological claim with scientific arguments. . . .

Finally, there are those who argue against cloning based on the perception that it will harm society at large in some way. The *New York Times* columnist William Safire expresses the opinion of many others when he says, "cloning's identicality would restrict evolution." This is bad, he argues, because "the continued interplay of genes . . . is central to humankind's progress." But Mr. Safire is wrong on both practical and theoretical grounds. On practical grounds, even if human cloning became efficient, legal, and popular among those in the moneyed classes (which is itself highly unlikely), it would still only account for a fraction of a percent of all the children born onto this earth. Furthermore, each of the children born by cloning to different

families would be different from one another, so where does the identicality come from?

On theoretical grounds, Safire is wrong because humankind's
progress has nothing to do with unfettered evolution, which is always
unpredictable and not necessarily upward bound. H. G. Wells recognized this principle in his 1895 novel *The Time Machine*, which
portrays the natural evolution of humankind into weak and dimwit-
ted, but cuddly little creatures. And Kurt Vonnegut follows this same
theme in *Galápagos*, where he suggests that our "big brains" will
be the cause of our downfall, and future humans with smaller brains
and powerful flippers will be the only remnants of a once great
species, a million years hence.

Although most politicians professed outrage at the prospect
of human cloning when Dolly [the cloned sheep] was first announced,
Senator Tom Harkin of Iowa was the one lone voice in opposition.
"What nonsense, what utter nonsense, to think that we can hold up
our hands and say, 'Stop,'" Mr. Harkin said. "Human cloning will
take place, and it will take place in my lifetime. I don't fear it at all.
I welcome it". . . .

Those who want to clone themselves or their children will not
be impeded by governmental laws or regulations. The marketplace—
not government or society—will control cloning. And if cloning is
banned in one place, it will be made available somewhere else—
perhaps on an underdeveloped island country happy to receive the
tax revenue. Indeed, within two weeks of Dolly's announcement, a
group of investors formed a Bahamas-based company called Clon-
aid (under the direction of a French scientist named Dr. Brigitte Bois-
selier) with the intention of building a clinic where cloning services
would be offered to individuals for a fee of $200,000. According to
the description provided on their web page (http://www.clonaid.
com), they plan to offer "a fantastic opportunity to parents with
fertility problems or homosexual couples to have a child cloned from
one of them."

Irrespective of whether this particular venture actually succeeds, others will certainly follow. For in the end, international borders can do little to impede the reproductive practices of couples and
individuals.

—Lee M. Silver, from *Remaking Eden: How Genetic Engineering
and Cloning Will Transform the American Family.*

1. Explain or look up the meaning of these words: *the Vatican, protocol, embryo, reprogenetic, theological, unfettered, impeded.*

2. Is Silver for or against human cloning? Explain why.

3. What objections to cloning from religious people does he mention?

4. How does he answer them?

5. What objection does he mention that is based on the good of society? How does he answer it?

6. What authors does he cite to advance his opinion? Why does he include two novelists in an argument about science and technology?

7. In his opinion, what will make it impossible for laws and governments to stop cloning and similar reproductive technology?

Guidelines for Persuasive Writing

When you attempt persuasive writing, keep the following guidelines in mind.

- **Be logical and fair.** Do not oversimplify or exaggerate. If you level with your readers, they will respect you and are more likely to be persuaded.

- **Support your thesis.** You will not convince anyone if you just keep restating your opinion. Do your homework: give facts, reasons, examples, testimony (other people's opinions), and personal experience to make a strong case.

- **Respect your readers.** They have the right to disagree and are not necessarily stupid or wrong if they do, so do not insult them. Consider the objections they might have to your position and try to answer those objections.

Which statement is more persuasive?

A. Sidney must be on a low-carbohydrate diet because he lost 20 pounds.

B. Low-carbohydrate diets help some people lose weight in a hurry; Sidney told me he lost 20 pounds in three weeks by cutting his carbohydrate intake in half.

Without evidence, Sentence A isn't a logical statement. There are many ways to lose weight. Sentence B is logical and focused, although one example is only support, not proof, of the general statement.

Which statement is more persuasive?

A. *Spider Man* is a great film; it set records at the box office during its first week.

B. *Spider Man* is a great film. The acting of Kirsten Dunst and Tobey Maguire is outstanding, the special effects are thrilling, and the plot has exciting twists.

Sentence A lacks support. Box office sales the first week do not indicate how good a film is, only that it is popular. Sentence B makes a claim, then backs it up with supporting reasons, so it is more persuasive.

Which statement is more persuasive?

A. Although a new sports arena will bring jobs and profits to neighborhood businesses, taxpayers' money would be better spent on improving the public schools.

B. Anyone who supports spending taxpayers' money for a sports stadium is irresponsible and stupid.

Sentence B offers an insult rather than an argument. Sentence A makes a more careful, though debatable, claim and backs it up.

Stressing the Argument, Not the Personalities

The Latin phrase *ad hominem*, meaning "to the person," refers to the gimmick of sidestepping an argument by criticizing the person making it. In political campaigns, this technique unfortunately works far too well, especially when it comes in the form of negative advertising about the opposing candidate's character. Such attacks, however, do nothing to weaken the *arguments* of the candidate, only his or her attractiveness to voters.

In argumentative writing, by contrast, we appeal to the reasonableness and good judgment of the reader, trusting that, in an academic exchange, evidence and logic will win out over personal attacks. Our goal is to guide readers to see the correctness of our position, not to vote for a candidate.

It is true that the way we respond to an argument is often influenced by what we know about the writer. That response, however, has more to do with whether we think the author believes what he or she says than with the validity of the arguments themselves. If reliable evidence shows that capital punishment does (or does not) deter serious crime, it should not matter who presents that evidence. What does matter, however, is how well it is presented—well-presented evidence is tight, clear, and without logical contradictions. A well-reasoned argument, unlike an election campaign, cannot be defeated by a verbal assault on the personality of the writer.

Approaching the Argument from Several Angles

An argumentative (persuasive) essay is different from a mathematical proof. Most argumentative writing involves social issues, political policy, academic questions, or psychological or medical controversies. Such matters are complicated and can be seen from different perspectives and supported with diverse kinds of evidence. Reasoning is crucial in argument, but logic alone is not sufficient to make a persuasive case in controversies over human problems. A debate about capital punishment, for example, may involve legal, sociological, economic, philosophical, and political arguments. If you can combine several of these approaches, you will make a more convincing case than if you rest your case entirely on one approach and ignore others. It helps to do some brainstorming, clustering, or cubing to explore the range of the topic and see it from different perspectives.

Researching and Presenting Supporting Materials

Researching your subject will always improve an argumentative essay. No matter how convinced you may be of the rightness of your opinion, research will probably turn up facts that either strengthen or complicate (or, on occasion, even disprove) your argument. Also, research will make you aware of opposing facts and arguments that you should not ignore. It is not always necessary to bring the counterargument into a persuasive essay, but doing so effectively strengthens your own position: Winning against a strong defense is more impressive that sinking baskets on an empty court. If you favor capital punishment, for example, how do you answer religious objections to taking a life? If you oppose capital punishment, how do you respond to the argument that the death penalty is the one sure way to prevent a killer from taking more lives?

When you find material in books, in articles, or on Web sites that helps make your case, be sure to present it properly. Chapter 14 covers how to use MLA procedures for quoting, paraphrasing, and constructing a bibliography. Never present material from a source by pretending that it is yours. If you use language from the source, use quotation marks and cite the source. If you use the facts and ideas but not the language, you still must identify and cite the source. Only general material that can be found in many sources can be presented without an identified source.

When you incorporate facts and arguments from secondary sources, use critical judgment. Statistics, for instance, can be very convincing but also very misleading. Be sure that the statistics you use are reliable and represent the situation authentically. They should be up-to-date, comprehensive enough to be convincing, and significant in what they reveal. If you quote authorities, try to choose ones with relevant credentials and an unbiased viewpoint. If you cite sociological theories or historical trends, avoid overgeneralizations and half-baked opinions. Irresponsible, immature arguments are seldom persuasive to informed readers.

WRITING TIP #13

Today's media are full of commentators who spout dogmatic opinions primarily for audiences who already agree with them. However, effective argumentative writers— political columnists, book reviewers, movie reviewers, sports analysts—are adroit, informed, and flexible. They are persuasive analysts rather than bullies with verbal clubs. Bellowing in a bigoted manner often silences dissent, but it will not persuade anyone who is open-minded. To improve your persuasive skills, try writing an essay from the other side: make as strong a case as you can for a position with which you disagree. You may learn something in the process, and isn't that what writing is all about?

Writing Exercises: Basic, Intermediate, Challenge

☐ Basic Exercise: Argumentation

Choose which of the two statements in each pair is more convincing and explain why.

1. A. The drinking age should be lowered to 16 because all college students drink already.

   B. The drinking age should be lowered to 16 because the chief harm isn't from drinking itself but from drunken driving and binge drinking by a small percentage of teenagers.

2. A. Lip syncing by singers in live performances and on television should be identified so that audiences know what they are hearing.

   B. Lip syncing by singers in live performances and on television should be legally prohibited because no one wants to hear a recording instead of a real voice.

3. A. Professional athletes should not be allowed to strike because they are not worth the money they are paid.

   B. Professional athletes should use strikes as a very last resort because strikes can shut down a whole season and harm the sport for years to come.

4. A. Young adults should never use medications such as anti-depressants or birth control pills because these medications sometimes have side effects.

   B. Young adults should consult a doctor before using medications that have possible side effects.

5. A. Penny's instructor graded her unfairly because she received a B while two other students with the same grades on their papers and exams received As.

   B. Penny's instructor graded her unfairly because she received a B even though she was never absent or late.

6. A. Weight Losers must be a better program than Scale Down because Hector used Weight Losers and lost five pounds while Donald used Scale Down and gained three.

   B. Weight Losers seems to be a more effective program than Scale Down because three studies show that 60% of Weight

Losers members lost at least 10 pounds and kept the weight off for two years, whereas only 10% of Scale Down members lost any weight after two years.

7. A. You can tell that the defendant is guilty because he looked shifty-eyed and nervous when he was interviewed on television.

   B. The defendant is probably guilty because he has no alibi, the gun was found in his possession, and samples of his DNA were found at the scene of the crime.

▣ Intermediate Exercise: Argumentation

Read the following passage and answer the questions afterward:

There are good reasons to oppose mandatory testing for drugs at the workplace and in schools. For one thing, it would violate the rights of citizens, because the Fourth Amendment to the U.S. Constitution protects people against "unreasonable searches and seizures." In places of employment, it would be an invasion of privacy for workers to be forced to take drug tests, and in educational institutions it would create a frightening atmosphere for students who should have a positive, trusting attitude toward their schools. Furthermore, testing is not foolproof and could create false accusations against workers or students, who in some cases could sue companies and school systems for millions of dollars. The cost of administering reliable drug tests would be exorbitant to begin with. In addition, the argument that drug use is widespread and is causing harm to businesses and schools is not entirely adequate, since there are many other patterns of behavior, including petty crime, abuse of legal substances, bullying, and sexual harassment that occur. For these equally harmful practices no one is proposing that all workers and students, most of whom are innocent of such behavior, must be tested or investigated in some way because of the bad actions of a few.

1. Identify an example of citing an authority in this passage.

2. Identify an example of an argument discussing consequences of the proposed action.

3. Identify an argument made by the opposing side that this writer rebuts.

4. Explain an economic argument used in this passage.

5. Explain which argument you find to be strongest and which you find to be weakest.

6. Explain what kind of personal example could be used to support the argument made in this passage.

7. State an argument that you think would further strengthen this passage.

■ Challenge Exercise: Argumentation

Write responses to the following instructions:

1. Give two arguments in favor of capital punishment and two against it.

2. Give one economic reason and one medical reason for (or against) legalizing marijuana.

3. Explain what kind of statistics would be useful in supporting or opposing the construction of a large sports stadium in your city or town.

4. Explain what kinds of experts could be quoted to support or oppose legal abortion.

5. Identify which part or parts of the U.S. Constitution are relevant to an argument for or against holding suspected terrorists without trial.

6. Identify what examples you might use to argue for or against changing the method of voting in United States elections.

7. Describe a personal experience of your own you might use to support or oppose increased testing of school children throughout the United States.

Essay Topics: Argumentation

Write an essay in which you agree or disagree with one of the following statements. Base your argument not only on your own analysis and opinions but also on support from material found on the Web and in the library. Narrow the topic if necessary.

1. The threat of terrorism requires Americans to give up some of our civil liberties.

2. The United States has the capacity to help other countries fight the AIDS crisis.

3. Nationwide testing is having a beneficial effect on American education.

4. Films based on novels are usually not as good as the books.

5. Marriage should be redefined to include gay couples.

6. Home schooling is providing better education than public schools.

7. The use of performance enhancing substances should be made legal in sports.

PEER REVIEW QUESTIONS: ARGUMENTATION

1. In your essay, you are trying to convince me that:

2. Your introduction is interesting.   ☐ yes   ☐ no
   Your introduction makes the purpose of your essay clear.
   ☐ yes   ☐ no
   The sentence that most nearly expresses your main point is the following:

3. You offer the following supporting arguments to back up your main point:

4. Your method of argument seems fair, logical, and persuasive, and you use more than one way to support your point.   ☐ yes   ☐ no

5. Your conclusion (is/is not) effective for the following reason:

6. What I like best about your essay is the following:

7. I recommend you make the following changes:

Proofreading Practice: Sentence Combining

Argumentative or persuasive writing often requires you to construct complicated sentences. To improve your sentence-forming skills, practice sentence combining. To develop variety in the kinds of sentences you write, practice combining shorter statements into more complex sentences. You can combine short elements of sentences in various ways.

For example, we can combine the following basic sentences in several ways.

Rosa woke up.

She got out of bed.

She got dressed quickly.

She ate breakfast.

She left for work.

One way is to write this as a single sentence:

After waking up and getting out of bed, Rosa got dressed quickly, ate breakfast, and left for work.

Here is another:

Rosa woke up, got out of bed and dressed quickly; then she ate breakfast and left for work.

And a third:

Rosa, after waking up, got out of bed, dressed quickly, and ate breakfast; then she left for work.

Can you think of another way?

After you have written a complete draft of any essay, but especially an argumentative essay, revise some of your sentences to avoid monotonous repetition of patterns. If one sentence after another follows the subject-verb-object pattern, try varying the beginnings of your sentences as well as their overall structure.

TEST YOURSELF: SENTENCE COMBINING

Combine the following basic sentence elements into no more than two well-shaped sentences. Do the exercise in two different ways.

1. Helen lost her watch.

2. She looked for it in the car.

3. She looked for it in her purse.

4. She looked for it in her apartment.

5. She finally gave up looking.

6. She bought a new watch.

7. Then she found the old one in her desk.

Answers: (two possibilities; try your own): 1. Helen lost her watch and looked for it in the car, in her purse, and in her apartment. Finally, she gave up looking and bought a new watch; then she found the old one in her desk. 2. Having lost her watch, Helen looked for it in the car, in her purse, and in her apartment. After giving up looking, she bought a new watch, only to find the old one in her desk.

Proofreading Exercises: Basic, Intermediate, Challenge

☐ Basic Exercise: Sentence Combining

Combine the following basic sentence elements into no more than two well-shaped sentences. Try to do the exercise in two different ways.

1. Rafael wanted a job.

2. The job would be in sales.

3. He looked in the want ads.

4. He stopped at the placement office.

5. He did a Web search.

6. He found six openings.

7. He applied for two of them.

▪ Intermediate Exercise: Sentence Combining

Combine the following basic sentence elements into no more than two well-shaped sentences. Try to do the exercise in two different ways.

1. The first year of college is exciting.

2. It forces you to schedule your time.

3. You meet new classmates.

4. You try new activities.

5. You explore new subjects.

6. You make major decisions.

7. It causes you to become a new person.

■ Challenge Exercise: Sentence Combining

Combine the following basic sentence elements into no more than two well-shaped sentences. Try to do the exercise in two different ways.

1. Learning a new language requires patience.

2. It takes time.

3. You learn new grammatical concepts.

4. You learn new kinds of pronunciation.

5. You acquire aspects of a different culture.

6. It improves your memory.

7. It also helps you to understand English.

CHAPTER 14
WRITING A RESEARCH PAPER

Making Sense of Sources

Writing about academic subjects often requires you to do research using library and Internet sources and to make intelligent and correct use of material from books, articles, and Web sites. Your professors will tell you whether they want an assignment to be entirely your own analysis and opinions or whether they want you to use researched information to augment your views. Essays about literature, for example, are done both ways. Often instructors want students to do as much of their own thinking about a play, poem, or story as possible and prefer that they not use secondary sources. Some papers on literature, however, are greatly enriched by the use of biographical, historical, and critical sources.

To use research well, familiarize yourself with the two chief ways of presenting source material: paraphrasing and quoting. And find out about the different formats for research papers in different disciplines. The two most common are MLA (Modern Language Association) format, used in the humanities, and APA (American Psychological Association) format, used in the social sciences. The MLA's style book is the *MLA Handbook for Writers of Research Papers*, 5th ed.; information about MLA format also can be found at the MLA's Web site, www.mla.org, or at university Web sites such as the Purdue University OWL (Online Writing Lab) site, http://owl.english.purdue.edu/handouts/research/

r_mla.html. The APA's style guide is titled the *Publication Manual of the American Psychological Association, 5th ed.*, and you can get online information about that format style from the APA's site at www.apastyle.org/ or OWL's APA site at http://owl.english. purdue.edu/handouts/research/r_apa.html.

One note of caution about using sources: do not hide behind them. If you are good at finding interesting material on the Web or in the library, you will be tempted to just download it and dump it on the page. But that will not produce an interesting paper, at least not a cohesive one. Imagine yourself as a courtroom attorney presenting a case. Your source material is your evidence—the facts and testimony that support the conclusion you want your "jury," the readers, to reach. It is your case to win or lose; the factual evidence and what your witnesses say is crucial, but you are the lawyer directing the case. You have the first and last word.

Paraphrasing

Paraphrasing a passage from an article or book means reporting, or summarizing, *in your own words* what the passage says. *In your own words* means *entirely* in your own words, not a few of your own words, then seven or eight words from the article, then a few more of yours, and so on. You may have to practice to be able to paraphrase without using the author's own words and without changing the meaning. Here is an example of a paraphrased passage:

Original passage:

> Of the numerous achievements that distinguish Richard Wright's place in the history of American literature, perhaps none is more important than the fact that he was the first African-American writer to sustain himself professionally from his writings alone.
>
> —Henry Louis Gates, Jr., *Richard Wright:*
> *Critical Perspectives Past and Present*

Paraphrase:

> According to Henry Louis Gates, Jr., one memorable fact about Richard Wright is that he made enough money just by his writing to support himself, and that he became the first African-American author to do so (xi).

Notice that the paraphrased passage says essentially the same thing as the original *but uses entirely different words.*

Why do you need to paraphrase? When writing research papers in some disciplines, especially the social sciences, you will use many kinds of sources written in many styles. Using too many varied quotations would result in a babel of voices that would drown out your own voice. And, quoting passages word for word can be boring, especially when all you need is some of the facts presented in them. Paraphrasing also allows you to shorten the source material, so that, for instance, you can reduce several pages' worth of source material into a paragraph. Although paraphrase does not have to be a summary of the original information, it is usually shorter than the original.

Quoting: the Long and Short of It

Everyone knows how to quote short statements: put the words in quotation marks.

Example of short quotation (whole sentence):

One critic writes, "This story should have ended before the last paragraph" (Smith 117).

Be sure to introduce quotations as this one does, with a comma before the quotation, and be sure to close the quotation at the end. Then cite the last name of the author and the page number in parentheses, followed by a period.

Sometimes you will include only a phrase from the source.

Example of short quotation (phrase only):

One critic argues that the author should have "ended before the last paragraph" (Smith 117).

Notice that the phrase fits into the sentence smoothly and grammatically, with no comma before it or capital letter at the beginning of it. However, the source is still cited the same way at the end.

Common Mistakes in Short Quotations

Probably the most common error in presenting short quotations is forgetting to close the quotation with a second set of quotation marks. Another is to begin a quote without introducing it, such as *one critic writes*, or *Joe Smith argues*. Always introduce your quotations: Without this lead-in to the quotation, sometimes called an *attributive tag*, the reader is left wondering whom or what sort of person you are quoting. Still another common error is the failure to use the correct method of parenthetical citation. Notice that *the period comes after the final parenthesis*, and nothing but the author's last name and page number is put inside the parentheses.

Long quotations, that is, quotations of five lines or more, are set off from the rest of the text and are not set in quotation marks. After introducing the quotation (using a colon), indent the entire left margin of the quotation 10 spaces (indent twice as far as the normal indentation at the beginning of a paragraph). Place the period at the end of the quotation, then a space, and then the parenthetical citation.

Example of a long quotation:

One well-known critic praises Richard Wright's work as follows:

> Of the numerous achievements that distinguish Richard Wright's place in the history of American literature, perhaps none is more important than the fact that he was the first African-American writer to sustain himself professionally from his writings alone. Primarily through the success of *Native Son* and *Black Boy*, Wright was able to support, for two decades, a comfortable life for himself and his family in Paris. (Gates xi)

Common Mistakes in Long Quotations

A very common mistake made with long quotes is using quotation marks. Another is not separating the parenthetical citation from the end of the quotation. A third common mistake is not indenting 10 spaces from the left margin (the right margin should be at the normal setting).

Using the Library and Internet

The Internet and the library are not totally separate sources of research material. In fact, a very large part of what is found in libraries is available *somewhere* on the Web—if you can find it.

In coming years, more and more of the vast stores of printed material in libraries will be available in databases, so that, according to some, libraries with paper copies of material will become increasingly obsolete as research centers will be transformed into centers used primarily for accessing electronic materials.

But for older materials, especially those on topics that have been written about for 50 years or more, that day is still a long way off. For that reason, if you are researching a paper in a course involving historical materials, expect to use a university library or another substantial library. Although many articles are available online, you may not be able to access full-text electronic copies of books. In addition, when you find a section of the library devoted to books on your topic, you may enjoy looking through what could be several shelves of volumes devoted to your subject. This experience is a bit like scrolling through several screens of Web links on your subject, but can be richer and more substantial. For example, try looking at the library stacks in the section on Shakespeare, the Bible, Mark Twain, or the Civil War.

Searching the Web and using a library are both similar and different. Both require persistence and patience, as well as know-how. Libraries have their own computerized catalog of holdings grouped by author, title, and subject. Once you identify them, you have to go get them in the stacks or have the librarian get them for you. Web sites, of course, require searches by author, keyword, or title. They have the advantage of not being physically removable by a single user, like books that are checked out; on the other hand, Web sites can be unavailable for a variety of reasons, and some of them frequently change addresses and content. Books and articles can be photocopied, whereas Web materials can be downloaded or printed for your immediate use.

Analyzing Source Material; Evaluating Web Sites

Know the difference between electronic versions of printed materials collected in online databases and independently created Web pages. Many Web sources exist in large electronic collections that amount to online libraries containing newspapers, magazines, and journal articles from printed sources. These online collections, often called full-text databases, may be available to you through your college library or city library. If they are, you can rely on them the way you would print materials from the library. Material from independent Web sites, however, must be evaluated differently.

When looking for sources on the Internet, remember a few general guidelines:

- Check the source of Web pages: Is there an author or institutional sponsor? If an author, does that person mention qualifications or credentials? Can you contact that person? If an institution, is it qualified to give information on this subject, and does it have its own Web site? To check the source, read the Web address and look for a tilde sign (~) with a personal name after it. That indicates a personal Web site. If the domain of the URL is .com, it is a commercial site; if the domain is .gov, it is a government site. Other domains are .edu, for colleges and schools, and .org, for nonprofit organizations. Foreign countries also have their own domains, such as .uk for United Kingdom and .de for Germany (Deutschland). Such information will help you determine how valuable and reliable the material is.

- Assess the purpose of the Web page. Is it trying to sell you something, persuade you to support a cause or contribute money, or merely supplying information?

- Is the Web page up to date? Having current information is important for some topics, such as foreign policy, health issues (e.g., AIDS and flu immunization), and government programs. A page on AIDS that was set up in 1992 and never updated would be far less useful than a page that was updated last year.

- Try to detect bias in the information you are accessing. Many Web pages pretend to give you nothing but the facts but actually have a strong prejudice. Check facts against other sources to see whether any of them are in error or whether important facts have been left out. Remember that many Web pages have not been scrutinized and approved by authoritative experts or groups. Check to see whether links are mentioned on the site and whether the links are still accessible. Do they also seem reliable and unbiased?

- Look at sites that can help you become an experienced evaluator of Internet sites, such as the following:

   www.lib.berkeley.edu/TeachingLib/Guides/Internet/
   Evaluate.html

   www.library.jhu.edu/researchhelp/general/evaluating/index
   .html

   http://lib.nmsu.edu/instruction/evalcrit.html

   www.library.cornell.edu/olinuris/ref/research/webcrit.html

   www.ithaca.edu/library/Training/hott.html

Avoiding Plagiarism

Plagiarism means using words, ideas, music, or art of someone else as your own. In a research paper you'll make use of many sources, but you will present them as belonging to someone else and use the correct form for identifying them that way. You must learn the correct form, because you can be charged with plagiarism even if you do not cheat on purpose. When you cut and paste materials from Internet sites, for instance, it is easy to put them into your paper without identifying them correctly, in which case you are plagiarizing just as much as if you deliberately stole the material and tried to pass it off as your own.

Remember that **all source material in your essay must be documented**. This means, as discussed earlier, that quotations less than five lines must be put in quotation marks and followed by a set of parentheses containing the author's last name and page number. Again, long quotations do not require quotation marks but must be indented 10 spaces and also followed by parentheses containing the source citation. Paraphrased material—that is, facts and ideas from a source put into your own words—must also be followed by a set of parentheses with the author and page.

Is there anything in your essay that does not require a source reference in parentheses? Yes: any parts of the paper that express your own opinions, conclusions, or analysis will not need a source reference because you are the source. Also, information that is so general it can be found in many sources—such as when the Civil

War ended, where the World's Fair took place in 1964, or how many plays Shakespeare wrote—need not be documented. If you are in doubt about facts that seem rather general but more specific than these examples, cite your source. It is better to overdo your source documentation than commit plagiarism.

Writing a Bibliography

As mentioned above, you must end each quotation or paraphrased passage in the body of your paper—which is called "in-text"—with a set of parentheses enclosing the author's name and a page number. When citing Web sites in text, you may not have an author's name, or there may be no pages. When no author is listed for a Web source, which is common, you may instead list a shortened form of the title in quotation marks. Keep in mind that for in-text citations you do not need to cite the author's name if you have mentioned it in the previous sentence.

These carefully noted in-text references are meaningless, however, unless you list the works—each book, article, and Internet source—from which they were taken. This list of works cited is called a bibliography (or sometimes a reference list), and it's crucial to your research paper.

The works cited list should be placed at the end of your paper, and the entries must be in alphabetical order so that any reader who wants to find the source that you quote or paraphrase can easily locate it. The word that appears in parentheses after your quotations must be the first word in an alphabetized entry in your list of works cited.

Each category of research paper has a set of rules for bibliography form. In the sample paper below, you will see the form most commonly used in undergraduate essays, MLA form.

Ultimately, the organization, presentation of material, and development of ideas in your paper are more important than the technicalities of form. Nonetheless, whether you are using MLA or APA form, you are expected to use it correctly. You do not need to memorize all the rules of these formats, but consult the appropriate handbook or Web site, listed at the beginning of the chapter, to ensure that you understand the rules and apply them without error.

Sample Research Paper in MLA Form

The sample essay below is a brief model of a research paper in MLA format. Please note these examples of quotation, paraphrase, and bibliography form before writing your own paper.

Lip-syncing: Cheating or a New Art Form?

Charles Morelli

Television audiences across the nation witnessed Ashlee Simpson become embarrassed by a technological malfunction on *Saturday Night Live* in October 2004. Although she had sworn never to lip-sync her performances, there she was, caught doing it on a *live* television program. Naïve viewers were shocked, but those familiar with the music business already knew that few "live" performances nowadays are done without the singer lip-syncing his or her own (or even someone else's) vocal recording. The question is, should we consider this another scandal like steroid use in sports and insider trading on the stock market? Or do fans enjoy lip-synced performances so much that they don't care whether Madonna or Josh Groban is really singing, so long as they can see the performer standing or dancing in front of them? There is no simple answer to that question, but there can be no doubt that in many forms, lip-syncing is here to stay.

Weak efforts have been made to oppose the use of background recordings in place of what appears to be a live performance. In fact, as reported in *Time* magazine, two congressmen introduced a bill in 1990 that would have made it illegal not to inform fans that performances were being lip-synced. By that time, Milli Vanilli, New Kids on the Block, and Janet Jackson had already frequently lip-synced their performances ("Sync along"). And famous artists have occasionally attacked others for not doing pure live performances. Elton John criticized Madonna for lip-syncing her performances, saying that she should not have been nominated for best *live* act. He declared, "Anyone who lip-syncs in public onstage when you pay 75 pounds ($134) to see them should be shot" ("Elton John").

However, many others have come to the defense of performers who lip-sync, chiefly because almost everyone does it. As Gary Giddins, in an article in the *New York Times*, lists the many performers who have used lip-syncing already:

> Among other performers accused of moving their lips while a machine does the labor are Britney Spears, Luciano Pavarotti, Shania Twain, Beyoncé, and Madonna. (One performer who won't be accused of lip-syncing is Kevin Spacey, but everyone who has seen "Beyond the Sea" wishes he had.) As for performers who sing in tandem with prepared tapes or backup tracks, this page could no more contain their number than it could that of film actors with lasered body parts. It's a wonder anyone bothers to deny it. (A21)

Giddins goes on to say that many fans actually preferred for Britney Spears to lip-sync, even though she claimed she did not, because it produced a perfect effect (A21). And some music critics are not the least troubled by the practice. Mark Brown, in *Rocky Mountain News*, for example, declares, "Let's make one thing clear: There is no shame in lip-syncing in the music world. It's a necessary part of the job in many situations. The finest musicians in history have had to lip-sync at times." It is also true that performers cannot dance the way Madonna does and be expected do their best singing at the same time. In fact, a friend of hers defended her against Elton John's accusations, saying, "Madonna sings everything she can sing but, if she goes into a dance routine, she's got to dance; you can't breathe and dance and sing at the same time" (qtd. in Walls, "Madonna's Pal"). And one reporter insisted that in a halftime Orange Bowl performance Ashlee Simpson should have used a recording rather than let loose with a "quaky howl" that produced boos from the audience (Slezak).

However, Brown also insists that performers should not lie about the practice, saying that Ashlee Simpson's problem was that before she was embarrassed on *Saturday Night Live*, she had declared, "Personally, I'd never lip-synch. It's just not me." Another critic lays down some ground rules for performers:

1. Don't fake it.
2. Don't lie to cover up a mistake.
3. If you make a fool of yourself in public, don't compound the problem by doing a jig. (Walls, "Ashlee Simpson")

And there is the additional problem of the technological touch-ups in nearly all recording nowadays, techniques that are so highly developed that a recording studio can make a young star with very little vocal talent sound like a gifted singer (Brown). The public might legitimately object that anyone who becomes famous as a singer should in fact be able to sing.

Purists and traditionalists of course will continue to insist on hearing truly "live" singers and remind us that singers who did dance routines in old Broadway shows somehow managed to sing and dance at the same time, and opera audiences expect singers to act while producing wonderful live sound. Some music historians, such as Norman Lebrecht in his book *Who Killed Classical Music?*, will continue to lament what they see as the total commercialization of music. Still, there will always be limited venues where genuinely live singing is enjoyed. But make no mistake about it: when you go to hear your favorite popular performer sing and dance before an audience of 20,000, the audience will be live, but the singing probably won't be. And you just may enjoy it even more as a result.

Works Cited

Brown, Mark. "Is It Live or Is It Pop Music Fraud . . . Again?" *Rocky Mountain News.* 30 Oct. 2004.

"Elton John Attacks Madonna at Awards Show." The Associated Press. 4 Oct. 2004. 1 Feb. 2005.

Giddins, Gary. "Put Your Voice Where Your Mouth Is." *New York Times.* 29 Dec. 2004: A21.

Lebrecht, Norman. *Who Killed Classical Music?* Secaucus, N.J.: Carol Publishing, 1997.

Slesak, Michael. "Ashlee Simpson Booed at Orange Bowl Show." *Entertainment Weekly.* 5 Jan. 2005. 1 Feb. 2005. <http://www.ew.com/ew/report/0,6115,1014344_10_000.html>.

"Sync Along with Milli." *Time.* 18 June 1990. 1 Feb. 2005. <http://www.time.com/time/archive/preview/0,10987,970375,00.html>.

Walls, Jeannette. "Ashlee Simpson Just Paying Lip Service to Fans." 16 Oct. 2004. 1 Feb. 2005. <http://www.msnbc.msn.com/id/6329101/>.

- - -. "Madonna's Pal Puts Foot in Mouth." 7 Oct. 2004. 1 Feb. 2005. <http://www.msnbc.msn.com/id/6192392/>.

WRITING TIP #14

Avoid thinking, "I'll do that later." Students who succeed best at writing research papers work according to a plan and progress carefully through each step of the plan. Never try to throw a paper together at the last minute, a day or two before it is due. Give yourself time to do the work and keep these pointers in mind: First, if you do a lot of handwritten prewriting activities, move past this stage earlier for a research paper than for other assignments. Second, when you find a good quotation, keep a record of the complete information—Web site, author, title, and so on—*at the time*. Trying to go back and find it later will increase your work enormously. Third, advancing from a handwritten draft to a word-processed draft is much more complicated with a research paper than with other essays, so make this transition earlier than you would for other work. Finally, the technical details of the MLA or APA form require careful attention and can involve extensive revision, so use the style books to familiarize yourself with these formats. If you give yourself enough time and do every step of your research paper carefully, you will save yourself a lot of work.

✔ Research Paper Checklist

Before submitting your paper, be sure you can answer "yes" to all of the following:

- [ ] 1. Is your entire paper double-spaced, with no single-spacing or extra-spacing between paragraphs?
- [ ] 2. Is your main thesis stated clearly near the beginning of the essay?
- [ ] 3. Did you make transitions between paragraphs, especially between major parts of the essay?

☐ 4. Are your long quotations at least five lines and indented ten spaces with proper parenthetical reference at the end? Are all of your short quotations in quotation marks and do they all have parenthetical references after them?

☐ 5. Is your paraphrased material entirely in your own words but true to the meaning and facts of the sources?

☐ 6. Does every parenthetical citation begin with an author's last name or short title? Is each name followed, when possible, by a page number? Does that same name or title appear in alphabetical position in your bibliography?

☐ 7. Does your bibliography have the heading Works Cited, and are the entries double-spaced and in alphabetical order?

Writing Exercises: Basic, Intermediate, Challenge

☐ Basic Exercise: Writing with Sources

Answer this true/false quiz:

☐ true ☐ false 1. A short quotation must always be enclosed in quotation marks.

☐ true ☐ false 2. A paraphrased passage should not be followed by a source reference in parentheses.

☐ true ☐ false 3. APA stands for Association of Political Activists and is the name for a research form used only for political research.

☐ true ☐ false 4. A quotation of five lines or more should be indented ten spaces.

☐ true ☐ false 5. The entries in a bibliography should be in alphabetical order.

☐ true ☐ false 6. MLA and APA forms are the same for bibliographies.

☐ true ☐ false 7. Plagiarism is acceptable with sources that are not covered by copyright laws.

▢ Intermediate Exercise: Writing with Sources

Read the following passage and do the exercises following it:

> How shall we know the past, and how date it? What aids to our vision will help us peer into theatres of ancient life and reconstruct the scenes and the players, their exits and their entrances, of long ago? Conventional human history has three main methods, and we shall find their counterparts on the larger timescale of evolution. First there is archaeology, the study of bones, arrowheads, fragments of pots, oystershell middens, figurines and other relics that survive as hard evidence from the past. In evolutionary history, the most obvious hard relics are bones and teeth, and the fossils that they eventually become. Second, there are *renewed relics*, records that are not themselves old but which contain or embody a copy or representation of what is old. In human history these are written or spoken accounts, handed down, repeated, reprinted or otherwise duplicated from the past to the present. In evolution, I shall propose DNA as the main renewed relic, equivalent to a written and recopied record. Third, there is *triangulation*. This name comes from a method of judging distances by measuring angles. Take a bearing on a target. Now walk a measured distance sideways and take another. From the intercept of the two angles, calculate the distance of the target. Some camera rangefinders use the principle, and map surveyors traditionally relied upon it. Evolutionists can be said to "triangulate" an ancestor by comparing two (or more) of its surviving descendants. I shall take the three kinds of evidence in order, beginning with hard relics and, in particular, fossils.
>
> —Richard Dawkins, excerpt from *The Ancestor's Tale.*

1. Identify three terms Dawkins uses to explain methods used to study the past.

2. Paraphrase his explanation of one of these methods, using only your own wording.

3. Write a sentence in which you quote a whole sentence from the passage in which he explains this method.

4. Write a sentence in which you quote a three- or four-word phrase from anywhere in this passage.

5. Imagine you are writing a research paper in which you use at least five lines from this passage in a long quotation. Write an introduction and set up the quotation in proper MLA form.

6. Imagine you are writing a research paper in which you paraphrase this entire paragraph but summarize it in only three or four lines. Write this paraphrased passage with proper MLA citation.

7. Write a bibliography entry for Dawkins's book using proper MLA form.

■ Challenge Exercise: Writing with Sources

Find a page in a textbook in your own field of study and do the following:

1. Summarize the page in paraphrased form, using only your own words but accurately conveying the main ideas of the source. Use a correct parenthetical citation at the end of your paraphrase.

2. Write a sentence in which you state a fact or two from the book, being careful not to quote directly from the wording of the book. Use correct parenthetical citation at the end of your sentence.

3. Set up a long quotation of at least five lines from this page, introducing the quotation properly and using correct MLA form for a long indented quotation followed by parenthetical citation.

4. Write a sentence in which you quote a whole statement from the book, using correct MLA form for short quotation: quotation marks and parenthetical citation afterward.

5. Write a sentence using a three- or four-word phrase from the book, using correct parenthetical citation.

6. Write a sentence in which you agree or disagree with an idea stated in the book, being sure to either paraphrase or quote the opinion stated in the book and separate it clearly from your own statement of your opinion.

7. Write a correct bibliographic entry for the book to which you have been referring.

Essay Topics: Writing with Sources

1. Research the day you were born. Find newspapers from that day and learn what was happening in the world. Identify one issue of the time and write a short essay about it.

2. Choose a film based on a real historical event. Watch the DVD of the film and do research to find out how accurately the film presents the historical facts. Or choose a film based on the life of a real person. Watch the DVD of the film and do research to find out how accurately the film presents the biographical facts.

3. Research the controversy over voting machines. How reliable are ATM voting machines, and what problems might arise from using them? Are other methods more useful, and should online voting from home computers be allowed?

4. Research the requirements for a career you are interested in. Find out exactly what educational qualifications and skills you will have to acquire and what demands are placed on persons in that profession. Explore current controversies regarding the training for people in that field.

5. Research an important event that your family or ancestors were involved in—an immigration movement, a war, a great storm or earthquake, an accident, the building of a famous structure, an event in the civil rights movement, or the overthrow of a government. Try to determine how your family's experience has affected your perspectives on the event.

6. Choose a story or poem assigned in your class and read two or three more works by the same author. Look up comments by critics on these stories and gather information about the author's life. Write a paper exploring a common theme in these works. (See Chapter 15 for more on writing about literature.)

7. Explore the controversies surrounding an event such as the assassination of President Kennedy, the attack on Pearl Harbor, the White Sox baseball scandal in 1919, the Florida vote count in 2000, the impeachment of President Clinton,

the Watergate scandal, or the attack on the World Trade Center. Watch out for Web sites making irresponsible claims.

PEER REVIEW QUESTIONS: WRITING WITH SOURCES

1. In your essay, you are using sources to find out the following:

2. Your introduction is interesting.   ☐ yes ☐ no
Your introduction makes the purpose of your essay clear.
☐ yes ☐ no
The sentence that most nearly expresses your main point is the following:

3. I am (am not) impressed with the way you use your sources for the following reasons:

4. I am (am not) impressed with your choice of sources for the following reasons:

5. Your conclusion (is/is not) effective for the following reason:

6. What I like best about your essay is the following:

7. I recommend you make the following changes:

Proofreading Practice: MLA Form

TEST YOURSELF: USING MLA FORM

Correct the errors in these sentences. One sentence is correct.

1. One critic writes, "This theme of this poem is reality and illusion (Smith 46)."

2. Dr. Shirley Montgomery writes that "she has done three studies of this problem" (38).

3. Harold Smith states, "The history of that event remains vague" (Jones 139).

4. "The novel ends weakly," writes one critic, but it is worth reading" (Miller 227).

5. One biographer tells us that Shakespeare's father sold many properties (Greenblatt 61).

6. One sociologist asks, "Where can we find data to prove this" (Martinez 22)?

7. Most patients who took this medication, according to one source, improved (17).

Answers: 1. illusion" (Smith 46). 2. writes, "I have done . . . 3. (139)— wrong author's name 4. critic, "but it . . . 5. correct 6. this?" (Martinez 22) 7. name of author is missing

Proofreading Exercises: Basic, Intermediate, Challenge

☐ Basic Exercise: Using MLA Form

Which four statements use correct MLA form? What is wrong with the others?

1. Jason Miller writes, "The film fails to capture the style of the story" (26).

2. One critic says the book has a "fascinating but implausible plot" (p. 103).

3. Baroque music, according to one historian, emphasized structure (Callandra 59).

4. Jessica Smith writes, "Such a poem could not be written today" (34).

5. One economist predicted a major recession in 2007 (McDonald 83).

6. A standard reference work of the time failed to mention his name (449).

7. "Most of this poem is unintelligible, wrote one famous critic." (p. 77)

▨ Intermediate Exercise: Using MLA Form

Correct the errors in these sentences. One sentence is correct.

1. One reviewer called the film "an unequaled masterpiece (Smith 246)".

2. Harrison McTwiggle reports that "he found the book enchanting" (38).

3. Simon Carruthers writes, "That day she found her true career" (Simon 321).

4. "Reading a poem," the editor writes, requires imagination and precision" (Smith 13).

5. In John Adams' day, Harvard University had one hundred students (McCullough 35).

6. "Where do we find her equal today" one biographer asks (Ferguson 44)?

7. One newspaper editor complained that not enough aid had been pledged (p. A19).

■ Challenge Exercise: Using MLA Form

Correct the seven errors in this passage.

Ernest Hemingway's story, *"A Clean, Well-Lighted Place,"* portrays two waiters observing a drunken old man lingering in their café, not wanting to go home. The younger waiter is impatient to leave to go home to his wife. His more mature co-worker, who lives alone, identifies more with the emptiness the old man must feel. He describes himself as one of "those who do not want to go to bed. (32)" After the man leaves and they close the café, he stops at a bar, feeling empty and afraid, with the word *nada* running through his mind. Although this story, unlike several others which Hemingway also published in "Scribner's Magazine" in 1933, is not directly autobiographical, it does, according to one biographer, express the "underside of Ernest's spiritual world" (Baker 238). The story was well liked by Hemingway's editor, Maxwell Perkins (Carlos Baker, p. 241) at the time and remains one of his best known works. Later critics have continued to respond to the power of the story. Warren Bennett in 1970, for example, finds it "superbly charged with dramatic as well as verbal irony (79). And

David Kerner in 1992 finds the story to be a symbolic comment on the human need for a refuge, a theme explored somewhat differently in a story called The Gambler, the Nun, and the Radio," which was published in *Scribner's* the same year (pp. 573–4). The enduring relevance of "A Clean, Well-Lighted Place" is evident in the fact that it is often included in literary anthologies intended for study in college classrooms.

CHAPTER 15

WRITING
ABOUT LITERATURE

Methods of Interpreting a Story, Play, or Poem

Writing about stories, novels, plays, and poems requires creative and critical thinking at the same time. If you are not an English major and do not have much experience in writing about literature, you may feel incompetent the first time you are asked to interpret a short story or poem. Do not be dismayed—a successful essay on literature does not require specialized knowledge or technical training. Unlike other academic disciplines, the study of literature involves us as whole human beings; when you write about literature, you are responding to it as a whole person with life experience. Professional literary critics may be more familiar than you are with other works of literature and with terminology that is new to you, but what matters most about literature, its vision of life, applies to all of us, whether or not we are well read.

This means that your essay should come more from your genuine response to the story or poem than from an attempt to sound intellectual or sophisticated. You will impress readers more with your keen insights and authentic responses than by borrowing ideas and phrases from critics.

Student Essay: Writing about a Story

The following essay, like many written in composition courses, takes an approach that is sometimes called "reader response," that is, analyzing the thoughts, feelings, and associations brought up in the reader's mind when he or she fully experiences the story. This essay is a response to a short story called "Eveline" by James Joyce.

A Trap or a Home?

Jessica Stevens

James Joyce's story entitled "Eveline" is about a young woman who is unhappy with her family life and her boring job and wants to escape. She lives in Dublin, where she works in a store and brings home money that she gives to her father. Her mother is dead, and she is looking after two younger siblings. All these responsibilities add up to a heavy burden for her at her age, and she feels trapped by her situation. The story portrays her facing the biggest crisis of her life—a chance to elope with a sailor named Frank, who wants to take her to Buenos Aires and marry her. The way she reacts in this moment of crisis would make any reader feel torn between opposite feelings: I want her to run away with Frank and have a life of her own, but I also want her to stay and fulfill her family responsibilities. The author succeeds in making a reader feel intense ambivalence and think about what it means to make a life decision.

Eveline's situation is a sort of trap that she can't get out of. She has taken on family duties that there is no one else to pick up if she leaves. Her father, even though he threatens her and bosses her around, is getting older and needs her help more and more. She is looking after younger siblings, and more than that, she promised her mother before she died that she would try to hold the family together as long as she was able to. And with all of that, she seems to be a traditional Irish Catholic girl who must have grown up with old-fashioned ideas about her role as a woman. The idea of running away from all that would be frightening and make her feel guilty, but the idea of staying is also terrifying, because she imagines ending up just like her mother, who sacrificed her own happiness and ended up demented.

Eloping to Buenos Aires seems necessary if she is ever going to get away from the trap she is in. She is nineteen, which in those days meant she might be considered an "old maid" if she didn't get married soon. She isn't sure she is in love with Frank, but she likes being with him, and he really wants to marry her. She feels that this is her one big chance, and any reader would feel that too: if she doesn't do something now, she probably never will. At one moment in the story, I could feel her panic. Joyce writes, "She stood up in a sudden impulse of terror. Escape! She must escape! Frank would save her. He would give her life, perhaps love, too. But she wanted to live. Why should she be unhappy? She had a right to happiness." At this moment in the story, I wanted to stand up and cheer for her to take off and go with Frank.

But she doesn't go with him. She can't, because she is overwhelmed by her responsibilities and the fear of taking such a drastic step. What would people think of her? What would happen to her? James Joyce shows how people can be trapped by their fears and by the way they are conditioned by their upbringing. Most readers are probably sad when they realize that Eveline can't break away from her dead-end job and boring life. Her home has become a trap that she can never escape from. But her trap is the only home she knows, and she has some good feelings about her family. Some readers would probably say she does the right thing. The ending of the story makes you feel sorry for Eveline but you accept her for who she is.

---

1. What does Jessica like about this story?

2. What feelings does she say it calls up in the reader? What does *ambivalence* mean?

3. What is the thesis statement of the essay? How is it reinforced in the conclusion?

4. What verb tense does Jessica use in discussing the story? Why is this correct?

5. What is the purpose of the quotation from the story in paragraph three?

6. What's the significance of the title of Jessica's essay?

7. Does Jessica give a balanced or biased view of the conflict between individual happiness and social responsibility?

Example by a Published Author:
Writing about Poetry

Published literary critics usually analyze fiction and poetry using a critical method or theory and a wide knowledge of both the writer's work and the work of hundreds of other authors and critics. Always read stories and poems and experience them for yourself before reading the commentaries of critics. Literature is to be experienced, and your interpretation of it should grow out of your direct experience of reading it for yourself. Afterward, it can be extremely valuable to read what well-informed critics say about it. They will often point out things you missed and provide information about the author's life and work that you may not know.

The analysis below is by critic Paula Bennett, who is writing about a poem by Emily Dickinson. Bennett brings to her analysis both feminist theory and a wide knowledge of Dickinson's life and works, as well as the writings of many other poets. This passage is from Bennett's book, which takes its title, *My Life A Loaded Gun*, from one of Dickinson's poems.

Emily Dickinson's "My Life had stood— a Loaded Gun"

Paula Bennett

Lacking the male poet's long-established tradition of self-exploration and self-validation, women poets in our culture have been torn between restrictive definitions of what a woman is and their own fears of being or seeming unwomanly. As a result, they have been unable to allow the full truth of their experience to empower their speaking voice. Without predecessors to whom they might appeal or upon whom they might model themselves, they have either fit into the existing masculinist tradition, or they have worked within a subcultural tradition of their own— the literature of the "poetess." In either case, they have inevitably been led *to dissociate the concept of creative power from their woman selves*. Though often possessed, as in Bishop's case, of extraordinary gifts, they have rarely felt these gifts as inherently theirs.

For the woman to exercise her creativity to the fullest, she must first be able to heal the internal divisions that have historically distorted and controlled her relationship to her craft. The acceptance of the self, whatever that self is, is the base upon which the woman poet must work, the source of her greatest authority and strength. But for her to arrive at this self-acceptance, she must possess a definition of her womanhood that is broad enough, flexible enough, to encompass all that she actually is. Without such a definition, she can never fully own her powers or achieve in her poetry the depth and scope of which her experience might otherwise make her capable. Burdened with ambivalence and self-doubt, like too many creative women in every field, she will remain a stranger to herself and to other women.

No poem written by a woman poet more perfectly captures the nature, the difficulties, and the risks involved in this task of self-redefinition and self-empowerment than the poem that stands at the center of this book, Emily Dickinson's brilliant and enigmatic "My Life had stood—a Loaded Gun":

> My Life had stood—a Loaded Gun—
> In Corners—till a Day
> The owner passed—identified—
> And carried Me away—
>
> And now We roam in Sovereign Woods—
> And now We hunt the Doe—
> And every time I speak for Him—
> The Mountains straight reply—
>
> And do I smile, such cordial light
> Upon the Valley glow—
> It is as a Vesuvian face
> Had let it's pleasure through—
>
> And when at Night—Our good Day done—
> I guard My Master's Head—
> 'Tis better than the Eider-Duck's
> Deep Pillow—to have shared—
>
> To foe of His—I'm deadly foe—
> None stir the second time—

On whom I lay a Yellow Eye—
Or an emphatic Thumb—

Though I than He—may longer live
He longer must—than I—
For I have but the power to kill,
Without—the power to die—

(no. 754; p. 574)

Composed during the period when Dickinson had reached the height of her poetic prowess, "My Life had stood" represents the poet's most extreme attempt to characterize the Vesuvian nature of the power or art which she believed was hers. Speaking through the voice of a gun, Dickinson presents herself in this poem as everything "woman" is not: cruel not pleasant, hard not soft, emphatic not weak, one who kills not one who nurtures.

—Paula Bennett, from *My Life, A Loaded Gun.*

1. Explain or look up these words: *predecessors, subcultural, ambivalence, enigmatic, Vesuvian.*
2. What special problem do women poets face, according to Bennett?
3. What does she mean by saying that a female poet may remain a "stranger to herself"?
4. What does Bennett mean when she says the poem captures the female poet's "self-redefinition"?
5. Bennett mentions that Dickinson speaks "through the voice of a gun." She sees this as a metaphor for the "Vesuvian" nature of Dickinson's poetry. Explain what Bennett means by her interpretation of the metaphor.
6. Bennett gives a feminist reading of the poem. Can you interpret the poem in any other way, one that might include all readers, not just women poets?
7. What effect does Dickinson's unusual punctuation have on your experience of the poem?

Analyzing vs. Paraphrasing

Many students, not knowing what to say about a story, take the easy route and simply summarize the plot. Once you head down that road, you can write a page or two without saying anything important. Assume that your readers have already read the story; in that case, what good does it do to tell them what they already know?

What can you say about a story, instead? Begin with *why* questions: Why do the characters act the way they do? Why does the author set the story in the place and time it occurs? Why do the events happen as they do? Why does the ending occur, given the situation and previous events in the plot? In addition, look for what is *not* said. We are often told to "read between the lines," that is, to draw conclusions based on what is said and done in a story. Authors rarely tell us in so many words the meaning or meanings of their works; literature requires us to respond with emotion and imagination so that we understand what is not said, as well as what is. A simple example is that an author almost never *tells* us that a bad character is bad; instead, the character does and says things that we dislike and disapprove of. The author does not *tell* us to admire a certain character, but rather, evokes our admiration by describing the courageous and generous things she does.

Developing a Point by Using the Text

In order to avoid the trap of plot summarizing, organize your essay in some pattern other than a narrative. Illustration or enumeration is one practical way to organize such an essay. If you want to prove that a story is about selfishness, elaborate on three or four examples of selfish behavior and their consequences, using a different paragraph for each example. If you want to argue that a story warns us against not standing up for ourselves as individuals, identify three or four negative consequences of meek conformity.

When you write about a poem, go beyond what the poem *says*. If you do not feel qualified to write about poetry, you will be tempted to paraphrase the poem and stop there. But, as with stories, assume that your readers have read the poem and that you want to reveal something they do not already know. What can you say about a poem?

Begin by noticing details: Poetry is about details. First, notice the language: Is there anything unusual about the language of the poem? Is it conversational, formal, full of suggested and hidden meanings? Also notice images: Do the images of things follow a pattern—are they of animals, plants, weather, clothes, money, food? What about the tone of the poem? Is it humorous, solemn, sarcastic, matter-of-fact? Does it change?

Above all, poetry works through double meanings and figures of speech—or as poet Robert Frost said, saying something by saying something else. When you write about a poem, explore the possible meanings of symbols, metaphors, and words that have multiple meanings. Interpreting a poem well requires almost as much creativity as writing a poem.

WRITING TIP #15

Writing about literature requires a kind of balance. At one extreme is the idea that every text has only one meaning, and that you must find that meaning, as if finding an answer to a math problem. At the other extreme is the notion that all opinions are equally valid, and that anything interesting you can say about a poem, story, or play is just as good as any other opinion. Interpreting and writing *effectively* about literature requires balancing these extremes.

Most works of literature have a few dominant ideas, or themes. A poet may express love, admire courage, lament the loss of life in war, or convey nostalgia over past experiences. Missing these predominant ideas and feelings does a disservice to your reader, but overlooking other meanings and reducing the work to one idea is just as unhelpful. A poem may express love and hate at the same time, or admire heroism in war but lament the loss of life, and so on. A good reader is open to a literary work's complex ideas and feelings while remaining true to its text.

Writing Exercises: Basic, Intermediate, Challenge

☐ Basic Exercise: Writing about Literature

Read the poem below and write brief answers to the questions afterward.

The Road Not Taken

Two roads diverged in a yellow wood,
And sorry I could not travel both
And be one traveler, long I stood
And looked down one as far as I could
To where it bent in the undergrowth;

Then took the other, as just as fair,
And having perhaps the better claim,
Because it was grassy and wanted wear;
Though as for that the passing there
Had worn them really about the same,

And both that morning equally lay
In leaves no step had trodden black.
Oh, I kept the first for another day!
Yet knowing how way leads on to way,
I doubted if I should ever come back..

I shall be telling this with a sigh
Somewhere ages and ages hence:
Two roads diverged in a wood, and I—
I took the one less traveled by,
And that has made all the difference.

—Robert Frost, 1916

1. Describe the situation faced by the speaker in the poem.

2. Describe precisely his response to the situation.

3. Describe the natural setting in the poem.

4. Explain the metaphorical meaning of the choice of roads.

5. Identify a line that contains more than one meaning.

6. Identify at least two emotions expressed in the poem.

7. Tell about a situation in your life where you had to choose
between two "roads."

▨ Intermediate Exercise: Writing about Literature

Read the following story and write brief answers to the questions
afterward.

War
Luigi Pirandello, 1939

The passengers who had left Rome by the night express had had to
stop until dawn at the small station of Fabriano in order to continue
their journey by the small old-fashioned local joining the main line
with Sulmona.

At dawn, in a stuffy and smoky second-class carriage in which
five people had already spent the night, a bulky woman in deep
mourning was hoisted in—almost like a shapeless bundle. Behind her,
puffing and moaning, followed her husband—a tiny man, thin and
weakly, his face death-white, his eyes small and bright and looking
shy and uneasy.

Having at last taken a seat he politely thanked the passengers
who had helped his wife and who had made room for her; then he
turned round to the woman trying to pull down the collar of her coat,
and politely inquired:

"Are you all right, dear?"

The wife, instead of answering, pulled up her collar again to
her eyes, so as to hide her face.

"Nasty world," muttered the husband with a sad smile.

And he felt it his duty to explain to his traveling companions
that the poor woman was to be pitied, for the war was taking away
from her her only son, a boy of twenty to whom both had devoted
their entire life, even breaking up their home at Sulmona to follow
him to Rome, where he had to go as a student, then allowing him
to volunteer for war with an assurance, however, that at least for six
months he would not be sent to the front and now, all of a sudden,
receiving a wire saying that he was due to leave in three days' time
and asking them to go and see him off.

The woman under the big coat was twisting and wriggling, at times growling like a wild animal, feeling certain that all those explanations would not have aroused even a shadow of sympathy from those people who—most likely—were in the same plight as herself. One of them, who had been listening with particular attention, said:

"You should thank God that your son is only leaving now for the front. Mine has been sent there the first day of the war. He has already come back twice wounded and been sent back again to the front."

"What about me? I have two sons and three nephews at the front," said another passenger.

"Maybe, but in our case it is our *only* son," ventured the husband.

"What difference can it make? You may spoil your only son with excessive attentions, but you cannot love him more than you would all your other children if you had any. Paternal love is not like bread that can be broken into pieces and split amongst the children in equal shares. A father gives *all* his love to each one of his children without discrimination, whether it be one or ten, and if I am suffering now for my two sons, I am not suffering half for each of them but double. . . ."

"True . . . true . . ." sighed the embarrassed husband, "but suppose (of course we all hope it will never be your case) a father has two sons at the front and he loses one of them, there is still one left to console him . . . while . . ."

"Yes," answered the other, getting cross, "a son left to console him but also a son left for whom he must survive, while in the case of the father of an only son if the son dies the father can die too and put an end to his distress. Which of the two positions is the worse? Don't you see how my case would be worse than yours?"

"Nonsense," interrupted another traveler, a fat, red-faced man with bloodshot eyes of the palest gray.

He was panting. From his bulging eyes seemed to spurt inner violence of an uncontrolled vitality which his weakened body could hardly contain.

"Nonsense," he repeated, trying to cover his mouth with his hand so as to hide the two missing front teeth. "Nonsense. Do we give life to our children for our own benefit?"

The other travelers stared at him in distress. The one who had had his son at the front since the first day of the war sighed: "You are right. Our children do not belong to us. They belong to the Country. . . ."

"Bosh," retorted the fat traveler. "Do we think of the Country when we give life to our children? Our sons are born because . . . well, because they must be born and when they come to life they take our own life with them. This is the truth. We belong to them but they never belong to us. And when they reach twenty they are exactly what we were at their age. We too had a father and mother, but there were so many other things as well . . . girls, cigarettes, illusions, new ties . . . and the Country, of course, whose call we would have answered—when we were twenty—even if father and mother had said no. Now at our age, the love of our Country is still great, of course, but stronger than it is the love for our children. Is there any one of us here who wouldn't gladly take his son's place at the front if he could?"

There was a silence all round, everybody nodding as to approve.

"Why then," continued the fat man, "shouldn't we consider the feelings of our children when they are twenty? Isn't it natural that at their age they should consider the love for their Country (I am speaking of decent boys, of course) even greater than the love for us? Isn't it natural that it should be so, as after all they must look upon us as upon old boys who cannot move any more and must stay at home? If Country exists, if Country is a natural necessity, like bread, of which each of us must eat in order not to die of hunger, somebody must go to defend it. And our sons go, when they are twenty, and they don't want tears, because if they die, they die inflamed and happy (I am speaking, of course, of decent boys). Now, if one dies young and happy, without having the ugly sides of life, the boredom of it, the pettiness, the bitterness of disillusion . . . what more can we ask for him? Everyone should stop crying; everyone should laugh, as I do . . . or at least thank God—as I do—because my son, before dying, sent me a message saying that he was dying satisfied at having ended his life in the best way he could have wished. That is why as you see, I do not even wear mourning. . . ."

He shook his light fawn coat as to show it; his livid lip over his missing teeth was trembling, his eyes were watery and motionless, and soon after he ended with a shrill laugh which might well have been a sob.

"Quite so . . . quite so . . ." agreed the others.

The woman who, bundled in a corner under her coat, had been sitting and listening had—for the last three months—tried to find in the words her husband and her friends something to console her in her deep sorrow, something that might show her how a mother should resign herself to send her son not even to death but to a probably dangerous life. Yet not a word had she found amongst the many which had been said . . . and her grief had been greater in seeing that nobody—as she thought—could share her feelings.

But now the words of the traveler amazed and almost stunned her. She suddenly realized that it wasn't the others who were wrong and could not understand her but herself who could not rise up to the same height of those fathers and mothers willing to resign themselves, without crying, not only to the departure of their sons but even to their death.

She lifted her head, she bent over from her corner trying to listen with great attention to the details which the fat man was giving to his companions about the way his son had fallen as a hero, for his King and his Country, happy and without regrets. It seemed to her that she had stumbled into a world she had never dreamt of, a world so far unknown to her and she was so pleased to hear everyone joining in congratulating that brave father who could so stoically speak of his child's death.

Then suddenly, just as if she had heard nothing of what had been said and almost as if waking up from a dream, she turned to the old man, asking him:

"Then . . . is your son really dead?"

Everybody stared at her. The old man, too, turned to look at her, fixing his great, bulging, horribly watery light gray eyes, deep in her face. For some little time he tried to answer, but words failed him. He looked and looked at her, almost as if only then—at that silly, incongruous question—he had suddenly realized at last that his son was really dead—gone for ever—for ever. His face contracted, became horribly distorted, then he snatched in haste a handkerchief from his pocket and, to the amazement of every one, broke into harrowing, heart-rending, uncontrollable sobs.

—Luigi Pirandello, from *The Medals and Other Stories.*

1. Pirandello is well known as a playwright. Explain what elements in this story make it resemble a play.

2. Identify physical actions in the story that heighten the meaning.

3. Identify two opposing views regarding parents and children in the story.

4. Explain how the setting of the story on a night train and description of the characters hint at the attitudes and emotions of the characters.

5. Describe the fat man's characteristics and explain how they are related to what he says and does. Explain what opposing feelings are in conflict within him.

6. Explain how the woman's attitude changes in the story.

7. State the overall message of the story, if you can. Or, do you believe the author refrained from giving the story a single message?

■ Challenge Exercise: Writing about Literature

Choose a short story that you like and write brief answers to the following:

1. Describe the setting, explaining which details create a particular emotional effect.

2. Identify the main character and tell why this person comes across sympathetically or unsympathetically.

3. Identify the actions by the characters in the story that convey the meaning of the story.

4. State the main theme of the story.

5. Identify subordinate or conflicting themes.

6. Identify physical details, actions, or statements that foreshadow the outcome of the story.

7. Explain whether the author reveals his or her point of view in the story.

Essay Topics: Writing about Literature

1. Find two poems on the same theme (love, death, courage, etc.) and write a comparative essay examining the similarities and differences between them.

2. Find two short stories whose main characters face similar problems and write a comparative essay exploring the similarities and differences in the way the two characters face their problems. Then explain how you have dealt with a similar problem.

3. Find two poems you like that were written by the same author. Research information about the author's life and try to determine which poem reflects more of the author's biography. Write an essay explaining your findings. Do not forget to cite your biographical source.

4. Find a story that you like. Look up information about the author's life and write an essay explaining what biographical facts are reflected in the story. Be sure to cite your source correctly.

5. Read a play, poem, or story and look up two critics' opinions of that work. Write an essay explaining which critic you agree with more. Be sure to cite your two sources correctly.

6. Read a well-known play and write a scene of your own showing what happens to the characters in their lives after the play ends. Try to remain true to the characters as they behave in the play itself.

7. Find a story or novel that has been made into a film. Write an essay explaining how the story changes in the film version. Find two reviews of the film and explain whether you agree with the reviewers' comments about the filmmaker's adaptation of the story. Be sure to cite the reviewers' articles correctly.

PEER REVIEW QUESTIONS: WRITING ABOUT LITERATURE

1. The overall purpose of your essay seems to be the following:

2. Your introduction is interesting. ☐ yes ☐ no
   Your introduction identifies the work of literature by title and author and indicates what you are saying about it. ☐ yes ☐ no
   The sentence that most nearly expresses your main point is the following:

3. You make use of details from the work to support your point without merely summarizing the plot. ☐ yes ☐ no

4. You quote effectively from the work to support your points. ☐ yes ☐ no

5. Your conclusion (is/is not) effective for the following reason:

6. What I like best about your essay is the following:

7. I recommend you make the following changes:

Proofreading Practice: Quoting Correctly from Literary Works

When you write about literature, check to make sure you have identified titles properly. Titles of short works such as stories and poems should be set in quotation marks: Kate Chopin's "The Story of an Hour" or Shelley's "Ode to the West Wind." Titles of long works such as novels or plays should be italicized: Tennessee Williams' *The Glass Menagerie* or Chinua Achebe's, *Things Fall Apart.* Also check to make sure you have begun and ended your quotations correctly, remembering to put quotation marks before and after the phrase or sentence quoted, and to introduce each quotation properly.

TEST YOURSELF: QUOTING CORRECTLY FROM LITERARY WORKS

Identify the three correct sentences below and correct the other four:

1. One novel that pits man against nature is Hemingway's "The Old Man and the Sea."
2. *The Black Cat* is my favorite story by Edgar Allan Poe.
3. Cervantes' *Don Quixote* is sometimes called the model for all later novels.
4. Richard Cory, at the end of Robinson's poem, "Went home and put a bullet through his head."
5. *The Stranger*, Camus' famous novel, begins today my mother died."
6. Langston Hughes's poem entitled "Harlem" begins with the question, "What happens to a dream deferred?
7. Guy De Maupassant's story, "The Necklace," has an ironic ending.

Answers: 1. *The Old Man and the Sea* 2. "The Black Cat" 3. correct 4. correct 5. begins, "Today my 6. deferred?" 7. correct

Proofreading Exercises: Basic, Intermediate, Challenge

☐ **Basic Exercise: Quoting Correctly from Literary Works**

Correct the error in each sentence. One sentence is correct.

1. Edgar Allan Poe's poem, The Raven, is eerie and haunting.
2. Poe continually repeats the phrase, Quoth the Raven, "Nevermore."
3. Poe also wrote many short stories, including The Pit and the Pendulum.

4. In his story called "The Tell-tale Heart," is about a man who commits a murder.

5. In "The Cask of Amontillado" is a story about a man who seeks revenge.

6. The main character in this story says "I must not only punish, but punish with impunity."

7. Poe often portrays emotional disturbance, for example, the "excessive nervous agitation" of the young man in "The Fall of the House of Usher."

▣ Intermediate Exercise: Quoting Correctly from Literary Works

Read the following poem and find the seven errors in the passage that follows it.

We Real Cool
The Pool Players
Seven at the Golden Shovel
Gwendolyn Brooks, 1960

> We real cool. We
> Left school. We
>
> Lurk late, We
> Strike straight. We
>
> Sing sin. We
> Thin gin. We
>
> Jazz June. We
> Die soon.

In the poem "We Real Cool" by Gwendolyn Brooks is about a group of adolescents who like to hang out and play pool instead of going to school or working. The adolescent speaker in the poem brags, "We real cool. We/Left school. The poem is written in street language that expresses the lack of education and the hip attitudes of these young people, who "Lurk late" and Strike straight." The tone of the poem is swaggering and strutting, "We real cool." These young people are proud of the way "they like to Jazz June."

Although first published in 1960, the poem contains the kind of rhyme used by rap artists and slam poets later. The jazzy pause before the end of each line creates a syncopated rhythm, and most lines use alliteration, for instance in phrases like "Sing sin" and Jazz June." The poem, in other words, expresses the creativity of these young people as well as their spirit of defiance, both their boldness and their defeatism. After bragging about all their daring acts of rebellion; "Sing sin. We/Thin gin" they ruefully predict they will "Die soon."

◼ Challenge Exercise: Quoting Correctly from Literary Works

For practice in quoting from literature, do the following exercises:

1. Write a sentence in which you quote a phrase of three or four words from a story, mentioning the author's name and fitting the quote smoothly into the wording of your sentence.

2. Write a sentence in which you quote a whole sentence from a story, mentioning the author's name, introducing the quotation properly and beginning it with a capital letter.

3. Write a sentence in which you quote a phrase of two or three words from a poem, mentioning the poet's name and fitting the phrase smoothly into the wording of your sentence.

4. Write a sentence in which you quote two lines from a poem, introducing the quotation properly and indicating the line ending with a forward slash (called a virgule).

5. Write a sentence in which you include the name of an author and his or her poem or short story, mention the title, and make a statement about the work without quoting from it.

6. Write a sentence in which you include the name of an author and the title or his or her novel or play and make a statement about the work without quoting from it.

7. Write a sentence beginning with a quoted statement from a story or poem and concluding with your own words after the quotation.

APPENDIX
Punctuation Handbook

The Elements of Punctuation

The major elements of punctuation are commas, apostrophes, end punctuation (the marks at the end of sentences), semicolons, and colons.

Commas

Know the rules for commas, and use commas only as rules require. Putting in too many commas does more harm than leaving some out.

Use commas:

1. in dates and place names
2. in a series and between several adjectives in a row
3. to separate coordinate adjectives
4. after introductory phrases and clauses
5. before and after interrupters
6. before and after nonrestrictive relative clauses
7. before and after appositives
8. before short conjunctions in compound sentences
9. before and after persons spoken to
10. before and after contrasting parts

11. before and after direct quotations
12. in correspondence
13. to prevent confusion

1. Commas in Dates and Place Names

Put commas between the day of the week, the date, and the year, as well as after the year:

> She was born on Tuesday, January 6, 1975, and grew up in California.

It is not necessary to put a comma between the month and year if no day is given:

> A Tsunami occurred in the Indian Ocean in December 2004.

Separate a street address from the city and the city from the state or country, but do not put a comma before the Zip code:

> He worked at 199 Chambers Street, New York, New York 10007.

2. Commas in a Series and Between Several Adjectives in a Row

Place a comma after each element in a series except the last one; the comma before the conjunction (*and*, *or*, etc.) is optional, depending upon which style you are following:

> They ate sandwiches, potato <u>salad, and</u> pie for lunch.

> Or

> They ate sandwiches, potato <u>salad and</u> pie for lunch.

(Keep in mind, however, that most academic style guides indicate using a comma before the conjunction.)

A series can contain words or phrases.

Nouns:	Books, records, and magazines lay on the table.
Verbs:	We ate, drank, sang, and danced at the party.
Pronouns:	I think that you, we, and they all look alike.
Adjectives:	The letters were terse, hard-hitting, and factual.
Adverbs:	The Jets played aggressively, efficiently, and shrewdly.

Prepositions: The detective looked in, around, over, and under the safe.

Phrases: The company preferred sales managers who were cordial with employees, knew the business, and demonstrated loyalty to the organization

3. Commas Separating Coordinate Adjectives

Several adjectives in a row modifying the same noun are called coordinate adjectives. They should be separated by commas if you could put *and* between the adjectives in place of the comma: a large, comfortable room (compare with a large and comfortable room). Do not put a comma between the last adjective and the noun:

an <u>intimidating, overpowering</u> defense

an <u>enchanting, imaginative, subtle</u> performance

a <u>squat, talkative</u> official

a <u>large, hairy, playful</u> sheepdog

In the last example, you could put *and* between the adjectives: a large *and* hairy *and* playful sheepdog. When you cannot put *and* between adjectives, do not use commas:

a <u>fine old</u> chair (not a fine *and* old chair)

a <u>navy blue beach</u> towel (not a navy *and* blue *and* beach towel)

4. Commas After Introductory Phrases and Clauses

Put commas after most introductory words, phrases, and clauses:

<u>Well,</u> you can never be sure.

<u>No,</u> that is not a good idea.

<u>Otherwise,</u> the plan will work.

<u>A few hours later,</u> she began to cry.

<u>When you have finished reading the article,</u> may I borrow the magazine?

When interjections (single words such as *well*, *yes*, *oh*, and *ah*) and interrupting words (such as *however*, *otherwise*, *meanwhile*, *first*, *nevertheless*, and *consequently*), begin a sentence, they should be followed by a comma. Interrupting phrases, also called

parenthetical phrases (such as *of course, by the way, after all,* and *in a sense*), normally also take commas when they begin a sentence. Short descriptive phrases (such as *in a minute, after the game, next to the produce, along the railing,* and *during the performance*) are usually followed by commas, too. Sometimes, however, short descriptive phrases fit smoothly into a sentence and don't require the use of commas. Compare these two examples:

<u>After a 30-minute wait,</u> she saw the doctor.

<u>In the section behind third base</u> was a row reserved for celebrities.

In the first sentence, the introductory phrase has a pause after it and should be followed by a comma. In the second sentence, the introductory phrase is necessary to the statement and should not have a comma after it.

Dependent clauses (word groups containing subject-verb combinations) normally are followed by commas when they begin sentences:

<u>Although the pay was good,</u> the job was unsatisfactory.

<u>When she thought about the past year,</u> she felt pleased.

<u>Since you joined the faculty,</u> the students have been ecstatic.

<u>Because the message was translated,</u> we could understand it.

5. Commas Before and After Interrupters

Sentence interrupters, or **parenthetical expressions** (think of *parentheses* before and after a phrase), are separated from the rest of the sentence by commas. When they appear in the middle of a sentence, put commas before and after them.

Here are some of the common interrupters:

however	of course	as a matter of fact
consequently	by the way	for example
nevertheless	in a sense	in fact
to be sure	in my opinion	in the first place

These interrupters are set off by *pairs* of commas:

She knew, <u>by the way,</u> that the computer did not work.

The sound track, <u>in my opinion,</u> is exciting.

The new model, <u>however,</u> will not be available until March.

Descriptive phrases containing past participles and present participles (*–ing* verb forms) after a noun often serve as interrupters as well:

The captain, <u>puzzled by the strange blips on the radar screen,</u> cut the speed of the craft.

An immigrant stonemason, <u>hoping for steady work,</u> appeared in the office.

Adjective phrases that come after nouns are also set off by pairs of commas.

The instructions, <u>dense and hard to read,</u> gave them little aid.

Two fathers, <u>anxious about their sons' grades,</u> called the principal.

6. Commas Before and After Relative Clauses

Descriptive clauses beginning with *who, which,* or *that* are called **relative clauses**. Relative clauses beginning with *who* or *which* are sometimes set off by commas. The rules are:

Do not set off restrictive clauses with commas.

Do set off nonrestrictive clauses with commas.

What are restrictive clauses? Restrictive clauses contain information necessary to the meaning of the sentence (i.e., they "restrict" the meaning) and therefore should not be separated from the rest of the sentence by punctuation.

Example 1:

Students <u>who receive A grades</u> may skip the second course.

The clause *who receive A grades* should not be separated by commas because without it the sentence "Students . . . may skip the second course" means something completely different.

Example 2:

The essay <u>that won the prize</u> was about illiteracy.

The clause *that won the prize* is restrictive; without it, the sentence does not specify which essay was about illiteracy.

Example 3:

The town <u>in which the research took place</u> was in California.

The clause *in which the research took place* is restrictive because the sentence has no specific meaning without it.

What are nonrestrictive clauses? Nonrestrictive clauses are relative clauses beginning with *who* or *which* (clauses beginning with *that* are always restrictive). Nonrestrictive clauses add extra details to the sentence but are not crucial to the meaning.

Example 1:

Electronic mail, <u>which sends messages instantaneously,</u> is beginning to replace "snail mail," <u>which is what some people call the postal service.</u>

The clause *which sends messages instantaneously* is nonrestrictive because it merely adds information and does not change the meaning of the sentence.

Example 2:

Philip Johnson, <u>who designed some of America's most interesting buildings,</u> failed the New York State licensing examination.

The clause *who designed some of America's most interesting buildings* is nonrestrictive because it adds information but is not necessary to identify the subject, Philip Johnson, whose name is already given.

7. Commas Before and After Appositives

Appositives are phrases that come after nouns or pronouns and describe or identify them. They are usually set off by pairs of commas:

Arno, <u>the great cartoonist,</u> was voted America's best-dressed man in 1941.

Neil Armstrong, <u>the first man to step on the moon,</u> earned his pilot's license when he was 16.

Some very short appositives are not separated by commas:

The Emperor Nero <u>was a psychopath.</u>

My sister Karen <u>will join us.</u>

8. Commas Before Short Conjunctions in Compound Sentences

Use a comma plus a short conjunction to link independent clauses in compound sentences. The short conjunctions are *and, but, or, for, nor,* and *so.* Remember to put commas *before* them but not *after.*

Independent clause	Independent clause

1. The location was desirable, <u>and</u> the price was reasonable.
2. Efforts were made by the police, <u>but</u> no suspects were found.
3. You may pay by check today, <u>or</u> you may have the store bill you later.
4. The first group stayed in the city, <u>for</u> they wanted to explore the museums.
5. The passengers were not injured, <u>nor</u> was the boat seriously damaged.
6. Sally had visited Puerto Rico before, <u>so</u> she knew where to eat in San Juan.

9. Commas Before and After Persons Spoken to (Direct Address)

When you speak directly to a person, using his or her name in a sentence, separate the name from the rest of the sentence. Use commas in pairs unless the name comes at the beginning or end of the sentence:

I remember, <u>Maria,</u> how you looked in high school.

<u>Maria,</u> I remember how you looked in high school.

I remember how you looked in high school, <u>Maria.</u>

Many writers omit these commas and ignore the difference in meaning: "I remember Maria" is not the same as "I remember, Maria."

10. Commas Before and After Contrasting Parts

Use commas before and after contrasting phrases beginning with not:

The Red Sox, <u>not the Yankees,</u> won that series.

The weather was cooler, <u>not warmer,</u> than predicted.

The capital of Pennsylvania is Harrisburg, <u>not Philadelphia.</u>

11. Commas Before and After Direct Quotations

Before quoting a whole statement, put a comma after the introductory word *said, stated, asked,* and so on:

> He <u>said,</u> "This is the road to Seattle."
>
> She <u>asked,</u> "Will this book explain how to sell real estate?"
>
> The catalog <u>stated,</u> "This course includes intermediate algebra."

Put commas after quotations when the quotations come at the beginning of sentences. Commas belong inside quotation marks:

> "<u>After dinner, let's play Scrabble,</u>" Sue suggested.
>
> "<u>Don't leave any questions blank,</u>" the instructor said.

Short quoted phrases often fit smoothly into the sentence and should not be set off by commas:

> Trevor called his brother a "<u>universal genius.</u>"
>
> Joanne was often called a "<u>Britney Spears look-alike.</u>"
>
> Shakespeare called music the "<u>food of love.</u>"

12. Commas in Correspondence

In business letters and personal letters, the closing is always followed by a comma:

Business Letters	Personal Letters and Notes
Sincerely yours,	Yours truly,
Yours very truly,	Yours,
Yours truly,	As always,
Cordially yours,	Best wishes,
	Love,
	Yours,

In personal letters, put commas after the greeting:

Dear Janet,	Dear Mom,
Dear Tom,	Dear Grandpa,

13. Commas to Prevent Confusion

Occasionally, you may need a comma to separate words that might appear to belong together when the meaning requires that they be separated. Watch especially for prepositions (*in, around, over, through*, etc.) that appear to go with the words after them when they do not:

> <u>Inside,</u> the room looked bright and airy. (*Inside the room* is not a phrase to be read together.)

> Not long <u>after,</u> the candidates gave speeches. (*After the candidates gave speeches* is not meant to be a clause.)

> All <u>around,</u> the landscape looked lush and mysterious. (*Around the landscape* should not be read as a phrase.)

Apostrophes

Apostrophes are used for two purposes:

1. In contractions, where letters have been left out:

do not = don't

should not = shouldn't

2. In possessive forms:

's for singular possessives: Karen's dress

s' for plural possessives: four students' grades

Exception: plurals that do not take *s*, such as *men* or *children*, take *'s* in the possessive:

men<u>'s</u> hats

children<u>'s</u> games

Some common mistakes that people make when using apostrophes are:

Carelessly leaving apostrophes out of contractions: <u>dont</u>, instead of <u>don't</u>; <u>shes</u>, instead of <u>she's</u>; <u>wouldnt</u>, instead of <u>wouldn't</u>

Writing possessives without apostrophes: <u>Karens</u> dress, instead of <u>Karen's</u> dress; <u>womens</u> opinions, instead of <u>women's</u> opinions

Putting apostrophes in the wrong place: my <u>mothers'</u> attitudes, instead of my <u>mother's</u> attitudes; <u>its'</u> cold, instead of <u>it's</u> cold

Using apostrophes with personal pronouns: write <u>hers</u>, not <u>her's</u>; <u>yours</u>, not <u>your's</u> (Impersonal pronouns do take apostrophes: <u>everyone's</u> opinions; <u>somebody's</u> car.)

End Punctuation: Periods, Question Marks, and Exclamation Points

Use periods to end statements and indirect questions:

Statement: The store had a sale on January 2<u>.</u>

Indirect question: Sam asked whether the store was having a sale<u>.</u>

Use question marks after direct questions:

Is this book overdue<u>?</u>

When will you be back<u>?</u>

Why, if no one objects to the proposal, are we waiting until March to begin<u>?</u>

Do not forget to put the question mark at the end of long, complicated questions like the last one.

Use periods, not question marks, after requests:

Would you please send me an application form<u>.</u>

Would you please let me know if you are interested<u>.</u>

Use exclamation points after sentences that express excitement or strong feeling:

Get out of my sight<u>!</u>

Watch out for that elephant<u>!</u>

That was a fabulous performance<u>!</u>

Use exclamation points after single words or phrases that express astonishment or strong emotion:

Help<u>!</u>

Stop<u>!</u>

No more war<u>!</u>

Semicolons

Use **semicolons** to separate independent clauses in compound sentences when there are no short connectives.

> Children of illegal aliens often attend public schools; some states have asked the federal government to pay for the cost of their education.

> Buying on credit has disadvantages; one may overestimate one's ability to pay.

Semicolons, not commas, should also be used to separate independent clauses when there is a long connective word (a conjunctive adverb) such as *however, therefore, meanwhile, nevertheless, consequently,* or *moreover* between the clauses. Use a comma *after* the connecting word:

> Separate conference rooms are available for the two <u>meetings; however,</u> you may convene together afterward if you like.

> We have already sent you a <u>brochure; meanwhile,</u> we are awaiting your request.

Use semicolons to separate independent clauses with the word *then* between them. *Then* is not a short connecting word like *and*; do not put a comma before it:

Not: We always swim at four <u>o'clock, then</u> we do aerobics.

But: We always swim at four <u>o'clock; then</u> we do aerobics.

Use semicolons to separate parts of a series when the individual parts have commas within them:

> She had lived in Dallas, Texas; San Mateo, California; and Stamford, Connecticut.

> You will have to pass three examinations: a reading test, in multiple-choice format; a writing test, in the form of a one-hour essay; and a mathematics test, given on a computer.

Colons

The colon (:) is used to introduce something. Use colons after *as follows* or *the following* to introduce lists:

> She called out <u>the following names:</u> Roberta, Carl, Tracy, Janice, and Lamont.

Open the bottle <u>as follows:</u> press down on the lid, align the arrows, and turn lid to the left.

Use colons when you introduce a list formally:

The ceremony will proceed in <u>this order:</u> first the procession into the auditorium, next the speeches, and finally the presentation of degrees.

A reader can enjoy the book except for a few <u>shortcomings:</u> its unrealistic plot, its difficult style, and its improbable ending.

Use colons to separate main clauses in compound sentences when the second clause explains the first:

Joan approached the interview with only one thought in <u>mind:</u> she intended to show them that she understood the job.

Don't use colons after informal introductory expressions (*like, such as, including,* or the abbreviation *e.g.*):

Not: We ordered five books including: *Like Water for Chocolate.*

Better: We ordered five books, including *Like Water for Chocolate.*

Not: You need three liberal arts electives, such as: sociology, history, and literature.

Better: You need three liberal arts electives, such as sociology, history, and literature.

Not: You need to eat more nutritious food, e.g.: oat bran and citrus fruit.

Better: You need to eat more nutritious food, e.g., oat bran and citrus fruit.

Credits

Jane Jacobs. From *The Death and Life of Great American Cities* by Jane Jacobs, copyright © 1961 by Jane Jacobs. Used by permission of Random House, Inc.

Martin Luther King Jr. Excerpt from "Letter from Birmingham Jail." Reprinted by arrangement with the Estate of Martin Luther King Jr., c/o Writers House as agent for the proprietor New York, NY. Copyright © 1963 Martin Luther King Jr., copyright renewed 1991 Coretta Scott King.

Luigi Pirandello. "War" from *The Medals and Other Stories*, translated by Michael Pettinati. New York: E. P. Dutton, 1939. Toby Cole, Actors & Authors Agency.

Dudley Randall. "Booker T. and W.E.B." from *Poem Counterpoem* by Margaret Danner and Dudley Randall. Detroit: Broadside Press, 1966. Reprinted by permission of Melba J. Boyd, Literary Executor for the Dudley Randall Estate.

William Shakespeare. From David Bevington, Ed. *The Complete Works of Shakespeare*, 4th ed. New York: HarperCollins, 1992, p. 305. Reprinted by permission of Longman Publishers.

Lee M. Silver. From *Remaking Eden* by Lee M. Silver, pp. 141–145. Copyright © 1998 by Lee M. Silver. Reprinted by permission of HarperCollins Publishers.

Benjamin Spock, M.D., and Steven J. Parker, M.D. Reprinted with the permission of Pocket Books, a division of Simon & Schuster Adult Publishing Group, from *Dr. Spock's Baby and Child Care* by Benjamin Spock, M.D., and Steven J. Parker, M.D. Copyright © 1945, 1946, 1957, 1968, 1976, 1985. Copyright © renewed 1973, 1974, 1985, 1996 by Benjamin Spock, M.D.

"The Tunnel" from *Zen Flesh, Zen Bones: A Collection of Zen and Pre-Zen Writings*, compiled by Paul Reps and Nyogen Senzaki. Copyright © 1957, 1985 by Charles E. Tuttle Co., Inc. Reprinted by permission.

Edward O. Wilson. Reprinted by permission of the publisher from *The Diversity of Life* by Edward O. Wilson, pages 259–261, 271, Cambridge, Mass.: The Belknap Press of Harvard University Press, Copyright © 1992 by Edward O. Wilson.

Index